T0161982

Building Sensory Friendly Classrooms

to support children with challenging behaviors

Implementing Data Driven Strategies!

Rebecca Moyes, MEd

All marketing and publishing rights guaranteed to and reserved by

Phone: 817.277.0727
Toll free: 800.489.0727
Fax: 817.277.2270
E-mail: info@sensoryworld.com
www.sensoryworld.com

Building Sensory Friendly Classrooms to Support Children with Challenging Behaviors: Implementing Data Driven Strategies!

Book design by Composure Graphics
Cover and interior by Composure Graphics

ISBN-10: 1935567233
ISBN-13: 978-1935567233

Table of Contents

Dedication 5

Foreword 9

Introduction 11

Chapter 1: Understanding Sensory Dysfunction 15

Chapter 2: How Many Students Are Affected?
What Does the Research Show? 23

Chapter 3: Data-Driven Decisions 39

Chapter 4: Signs and Symptoms of SPD 57

Chapter 5: Strategies to Address SPD 71

Chapter 6: Creating a Sensory Room within
Your School or Classroom 87

Chapter 7: Self-Stimulatory and Self-Abusive
Behavior—The Connection to SPD 99

Chapter 8: Teaching Stress Management
and Self-Advocacy through Behavioral
Cognitive Therapy 119

Chapter 9: IEP and 504 Language for SPD 133

Chapter 10: A Behavioral Support Plan for
Children with SPD. 143

References 149

About the Author 153

Resources 155

Dedication

In the therapy center where I work, I have met some exceptional people who struggle with sensory processing disorder. They have provided for me the motivation to write this book. In particular, I want to thank:

The adults and children who have allowed me to share their stories within these pages.

My daughter, Kiersten, an OT-2-B! Thank you for our late-night chats and edit sessions. I love you, honey!

My little sister and best friend, Cindy, with whom I share memories of scratchy clothes, neon-orange bedroom walls, Swiss steak, zipper scars, and our other sensory nightmares. We've been through it all, haven't we?

To Braeden, our photo-shoot model and one special little boy!

To Sam, a terrific kid who knows everything there is to know about flashlights and clocks.

To Aaron and Alexa, my nephew and niece: They always make Aunt Becky smile!

To Chuck and Chuckie, for all their terrific computer expertise...I love you!

To Mary Pat Shattuck, autistic support teacher for Warren Area Elementary School in the Warren County School District, Warren, Pennsylvania. Thank you for all your support and for the great photos of classroom sensory areas contributed to this book!

To Wayne and Jennifer Gilpin, for their vision and dedication, and for giving a voice to this disorder.

A special thank you to OT Sensory Expert Paula Aquilla for sharing her time and thoughts about this book!

To Temple Grandin, for her inside perspective about SPD and her willingness to review this book. Thank you so much! You are an inspiration to all!

Thank you again!

This book will inspire you with strategies to do your job even better! Rebecca Moyes explains sensory concepts in ways that are easy to understand. She investigates the WHY behind behaviors, offers doable, practical strategies from more than one perspective, and outlines how to collect data to support the use of sensory strategies in the classroom setting. Case studies are used to illustrate the concepts and strategies.

Mrs Moyes shares strategies that will enable us to better support children with sensory challenges in our classrooms. After all, she says, the children are depending on us to help them! Let's rise to the challenge.

— *Paula Aquilla, B Sc, OT; author of*
Building Bridges through
Sensory Integration

Foreword
Why This Book?

There are many children and adults who report sensory-integration disturbance. Sensory dysfunction can be present in individuals with learning disabilities, autism, schizophrenia, and bipolar disorder, among others, but has also been found to occur in higher numbers in the mentally gifted. Many "typical" individuals also report sensory dysfunction. When these disturbances greatly interfere with one's ability to function normally, the need for diagnosis and intervention becomes critical.

Much of the research regarding how to address sensory processing disorder (SPD) is still sketchy. Today, a variety of techniques are being implemented in classrooms to help students with this disorder find relief from their symptoms and prevent problematic behaviors. However, the techniques are often applied by using "hit-or-miss" strategies. Data does not drive these decisions. To compound matters, the scientific studies that have been conducted with regard to sensory-integration therapy do not yield promising results in terms of helping students to rid themselves of their sensory-processing disability altogether.

What we do know is that if SPD cannot yet be "cured," then what remains for us to do is to accommodate the disorder so that problematic behaviors arising from the disability do not interfere with a student's learning or the learning of others. Many students will respond well to these techniques. For some, it may appear that with these strategies in place, their dysfunction will be normalized.

When a student experiences hypersensitivity to certain stimuli, he will often experience a high level of anxiety. Avoidance behaviors will be observed as he attempts to escape from the sensory input that disturbs him. As with any other anxiety disorder, it is necessary to teach the child ways to manage his anxiety so that avoidance behaviors do not continue. Further, for some children, it will be possible to gently expose the child to the offending stimuli in small doses, and then pair his ability to remain in environments with heightened sensory stimuli with reinforcement (rewards) that he finds meaningful. We can often achieve success with this method, referred to as *cognitive behavioral therapy.*

As we begin our study of SPD, it is necessary for the reader to know that because of the severity of their disorder, some students may have more difficulty responding to any techniques at all. That is why each implementation of a strategy should be *(a)* preceded by a period of data collection to determine a baseline of behavior and *(b)* followed by another round of observation and data collection to note whether the intervention has been successful. Some children will respond nicely, and noted improvement will be seen. For others, it will be necessary to try a variety of techniques. For others still, there may be no improvement noted, no matter what strategy is attempted. These children will function best under the tutelage of sensitive teachers who are willing to accommodate their disorder.

The author believes that most children can benefit from the use of self-advocacy techniques and stress-management strategies to function appropriately in the classroom. They will need to learn that although avoiding the stimuli would be the easiest thing to do, it will only serve to isolate them and exacerbate the anxiety associated with sensory dysfunction.

This book will assist the reader in discovering ways to accommodate the disorder *and* provide ways to teach replacement skills to the student.

Introduction

My awareness of sensory processing disorder (SPD) came as a child. I had difficulty with many sensory experiences, and finding out about SPD answered many of the questions I had about my own particular quirks. When I read Liane Willey's *Pretending to be Normal*,[1] I could certainly relate to some of the sensory experiences she wrote about! As you will see, I am someone who would have benefitted from sensory-integration therapy.

As a young girl, I found it difficult to copy motor movements. I attributed this to being left-handed and having to grow up in a right-handed world. By some miracle, I made the cheerleading squad in junior-high school (most likely because one of the judges was a teacher who really liked me). I had plenty of spunk, but very little coordination ability. It took me forever just to learn the try-out cheer, and frankly, I was shocked that I secured a spot on the squad! Thankfully, back then, not much was expected of a cheerleader in the way of gymnastics, because I would never have been able to do the acrobatics with the expertise of cheerleaders today. I dreaded practices and games because I felt so awkward compared with my cheerleading peers. I couldn't perform a cartwheel without looking ridiculous. Somersaults made me dizzy. The coach put me in the back row of the squad—the least visible position. I was relieved when the season was over, and I never tried out again.

I also wondered, on occasion, if my ineptness was caused by an accident that I had when I was two: I fell through the railing of our cellar steps onto my head. I was unconscious for a few minutes and dazed when I woke up. However, it was most likely not the accident that caused my sensory problems. Rather, it was the reverse: My sensory deficits probably caused the accident! I seem to have no awareness of where my body is in space. This makes me afraid of heights and causes a problem with depth perception, which is probably the exact reason the accident happened in the first place.

Later in life, I began to accept my awkwardness with some self-deprecating humor. One time, in my early 30s, a friend asked me to join a jazzercise class. I told her that I couldn't do it because I was a "klutz," and learning dances was just too hard for me. (I hated the disco era, and you can probably figure out why!) But my friend was relentless, and she urged me to go. A stay-at-home mom with two toddlers 17 months apart, I desperately needed to get out. The need for grown-up company overrode my fear of dancing. I still remember the puzzled looks of the instructor as she watched my awkward movements. I could do nothing except dissolve into a fit of giggles with my friend as I tried to master the complicated steps. The same thing would happen whenever I attempted to participate in a line dance at a class reunion or wedding. And, although the Village People wrote a great little song about the YMCA, the dance is not so great for me! Although my husband says he would love to take me ballroom dancing, I think he secretly knows that it would probably be better if I just sat on the sidelines and watched him dance.

My problems don't just come to light when I'm dancing, however. Watching someone like me get on or off an escalator or a moving sidewalk is something you may never see again! I just can't seem to time my movements appropriately. I stumble on, feeling terrified, but I try to look casual. I am mesmerized by folks who can pull a roller bag *and* talk on their cell phones, *while not holding on!* As I approach my 50s, and I travel to many speaking engagements, I no longer find these deficits humorous.

Sometimes they are downright exhausting. Rather than attempt to drag a suitcase onto an escalator and worry about whether I can navigate the whole process, I take the elevator.

As if all that isn't enough, I also have other sensory difficulties: I have a keen sense of smell and often get headaches when I'm surrounded by the aroma of perfume or when I have to stay in a hotel room located next to an indoor pool. The chlorine sends me into olfactory overload. Dealing with odors was even harder during my pregnancies. Often, it wasn't food that made me queasy—it was my olfactory sense. To compound matters, I dislike when people touch my neck or back in certain ways. Once, while pregnant, I had severe back pains. I sought the help of a chiropractor. He gave up trying to adjust my back, muttering to his coworkers that I was a "hopeless cause." He asked me how the heck I ever managed to even *get* pregnant—I was so tactile defensive, it was impossible for him to even do the adjustments!

I have other sensory issues, as well: I don't like the sound of whistling, and I like to have my own space. I really don't like the sensation of wearing panty hose. I am not stable on my feet, and I do not like bleachers, amusement-park rides, or carpets with busy, colorful patterns. At the end of most workdays, I am in need of a warm cup of tea, my fuzzy pink slippers, and a soft afghan because I am in sensory overload.

All my little oddities are a puzzle to my husband, who doesn't seem to have any problems with sensory stimuli at all! How envious I am of him! Over the years, however, I have noticed that he has become less quizzical and more emotionally supportive as he sees me struggle. He "gets it." As an example, when the movie *Avatar* was released, I knew that he really wanted to see it. I readily volunteered to go with him. He asked me, quite sincerely, "Are you sure it won't throw you into sensory overload?" Being married to someone who understands all my little quirks is truly a blessing! My husband is a teacher, and knowing all these things about me has helped him be more aware of his students' sensory needs, I'm sure.

I have a keen desire to help educators understand children with special needs. This is my fourth book for teachers and parents in the field of special education. Within these pages, I want to share with you the words, pictures, and ideas that can make a difference for a child with SPD. I hope you will enjoy them! More importantly, though, I hope you will find them useful. I'm a data girl. *Show me the data* has become my personal mantra. I don't want to waste your time or the time of your colleagues. Because I have been a classroom teacher myself, I know that there just isn't enough of it to go around. You have to be comfortable with the strategies I'm recommending if they are going to be effective in your classroom. And so, as we begin our sensory journey together, grab a peppermint candy (to keep you alert) or your soft pillow (to help relax you), and please remember this: There are children in your classrooms with deficits just like mine, and they are depending on you to provide the assistance they desperately need to be successful in your classroom!

Chapter 1
Understanding Sensory Dysfunction

Today's teachers are often faced with the challenge of educating students who may have one or more physical or mental disabilities. Often, regular-education teachers are provided with little or no training in working with such students, despite the fact that they are mandated by state and federal special-education laws to include them in their classrooms.

One of the least understood and yet highly prevalent conditions among students with disabilities is sensory processing disorder (SPD). SPD is the inability to process sensory stimuli efficiently. As human beings, all successful learning experiences come from our ability to process and make sense of the information that is derived from our seven senses. When we think about the endless bits of sensory input that enter our brains and must be processed instantaneously from every part of our bodies at any given moment—a whiff of someone's perfume, the sensation of our sleeve brushing against our wrist, the sound of a cough, the smell of popcorn popping in the microwave—it's not hard to see why our brains truly are supersonic sensory-processing machines! In folks diagnosed with SPD, however, one or more of our seven sensory-processing modalities may be compromised. They are:

- **Visual** (what we take in through our eyes)

- **Auditory** (what we take in through our ears)

- **Olfactory** (what we take in through our nose)

- **Tactile** (what we take in through touch)

- **Gustatory** (what we take in through our mouth—this sense works closely with our olfactory and tactile senses)

- **Vestibular** (This involves our sense of balance and the workings of the inner ear—it contributes to our sense of equilibrium and lets us know whether we are moving or still, upside-down or right-side up; also, it tells us how fast or slow we are going.)

- **Proprioceptive** (This involves the way our brain coordinates with our muscles and nerves so that we understand where our bodies are in space. It tells us if our joints are bending or straightening. It lets us know where all parts of our bodies are and if they are working properly. This sense is known as *the position sense,* and it works in tandem with our tactile and vestibular senses.)

In teacher-preparation courses, there is often mention of the value of identifying and adapting to the individual learning styles of our students. These learning styles always involve the students' senses, and some modalities will be stronger than others. For instance, visual learners benefit from a "show-me" teaching style rather than a "tell-me" teaching style. These students may have language difficulties or short attention spans. For such kids, *seeing* the information presented is often going to be more meaningful than *hearing* it.

We may also be more familiar with the student who enjoys tactile learning opportunities. Tactile learners benefit when they have opportunities to use their sense of touch. For instance, a tactile learner would benefit from having opportunities to manipulate objects in an educational setting. Examples might include using actual coins to learn to make change, manipulating the days of a daily calendar chart to learn about sequencing, or using prefix cards to match up with root-word cards. Use of task cards, computer activities, crafts, and electro-boards can also provide opportunities to incorporate the sense of touch into educational activities. (The author has provided directions for how to make an electro-board at the end of this chapter.)

Kinesthetic learners enjoy movement. They will learn their A-B-C's faster when they have an opportunity to play a hopscotch game composed of letters of the alphabet rather than having a visual of the letter(s) (**Figure 1**). They will be engaged during lessons that involve drama, pantomiming, or interviewing activities. These children often excel at athletics. They are performers who have a great sense of timing in their movements and in body coordination.

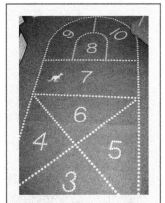

Figure 1. Changing the numbers to letters on a hopscotch mat, similar to the one above, may help kinesthetic learners master the alphabet.

In many schools, classroom instruction is primarily presented in an auditory manner, with little consideration as to whether or not this modality "fits" with the students' individual learning styles. In any one classroom, only a small percentage of students may benefit from auditory instruction. When a child's learning style is identified, and efforts are made to instruct the student via this modality, the child will be more engaged. This also holds true for a child who may have difficulty processing sensory input through one or more of his senses. If his sensory system is compromised, then we must tailor the learning strategy for him, as well! As an example, a child with tactile sensitivity may not be engaged in a lesson that incorporates tactile components.

> *Matthew disliked getting wet. He would overreact when his clothes became damp or when anything spilled on them accidentally. His art teacher was attempting to teach the students how*

to finger-paint. Matthew was asked to dip his fingers into the paint and draw a flower on a piece of construction paper. Matthew began to cry and shake his hands. The shaking resulted in his shirt becoming wet with paint, and this further agitated him. Eventually, Matthew had to be removed from the class.

When our sensory system is functioning well, we can be described as someone whose life is balanced. Imagine a waitress in a restaurant, who carries a tray high above her head, loaded with dishes. When we are able to process sensory input effectively, our "tray" is balanced. We are operating at optimal functioning levels and can accomplish all of our daily goals and tasks.

In contrast, when our sensory system is not functioning well, we may experience a heightened level of stress. We feel anxious and irritable. We may attempt to shut out excessive sensory stimuli by withdrawing in whatever way we can from our environment. We might be short-tempered or "on edge." Or, on the flip side, we may crave the sensory stimuli our body is not receiving. We may engage in self-stimulatory behavior to "rev" our systems up (such as hair-twirling, foot-swinging, and finger-tapping). Or, we could feel tired because we are not getting enough sensory input, and our world is bland and boring.

In some schools across the country, addressing sensory challenges has been recognized as belonging or pertaining to the domain of occupational therapy. Occupational therapists are often able to make recommendations for students who have sensory disturbance. However, the sheer numbers of these children make it impossible for occupational therapists to address the unique needs of all such students. It becomes even more critical, then, that educators understand how sensory deficits affect student performance and be ready and willing to implement support mechanisms for these students.

In some school districts and early-intervention programs, students with sensory deficits may not qualify for special-education programs. Such deficits are usually not addressed in special-education plans, and parents are sometimes told that these challenges are not educational issues. They are urged to find support for these problems outside of the school district. Many do. However, if the reason a child is exhibiting difficult behaviors can be linked through data collection to a sensory disturbance, how could an educator *not* address a sensory problem? All learning is accomplished through our senses! Therefore, any educational plan that does not take into consideration how a child learns is likely to be less effective than one that does.

When a child is hearing impaired or visually impaired, educational advocacy is usually not difficult. There are tests that can be used to measure these types of deficits, and we can clearly see the student's outcome as measured by his scores. As an example, if a child has difficulty hearing his teacher, individualized education plan, or IEP, teams are usually eager to provide the necessary accommodations and support. However, when we can't physically *see* a child's disability (ie, it is hidden from us), when it is impossible to measure or quantify it with an evaluation, or when we can't experience it for ourselves, it becomes very difficult to accommodate it.

Parents of kids who have sensory deficits often find themselves taking on not only the responsibility of advocating for support, but also providing education and awareness training for their children's schools. Children who have sensory disturbances need individuals in their lives who are willing to be flexible to their needs. These individuals should be folks who are willing to put accommodations in place that are different from traditional support mechanisms. These same accommodations may also require some advanced planning and involve some creativity and ingenuity on the part of the children's teachers and/or administrators to be successful.

It is the author's goal that this book will help teachers and administrators to understand sensory dysfunction and assist them in implementing some strategies that may make all the difference for one or more students in their classrooms. Additionally, the author will present information on how decisions that guide the selection of these interventions can and should be based on data collection and analysis. If data does not guide decisions, students with sensory deficits may become victims of experimental treatments that cause more harm than good in the end, and their teachers will have wasted valuable teacher-student productivity time.

Making an Electro-Board to Review for a Test

1. Obtain two press-board folders. Open up the first folder. On one side of the folder, write the review questions and number them. Allow a little bit of space between each question.

2. Using a hole-puncher, punch a small hole either before the question number or after the question itself.

3. Insert a brass brad into each hole.

4. On the opposite side of the folder, write the answers to the questions by using A-Z. Do not put them in the correct order.

5. Using a hole-puncher, punch a small hole either before the answer letter or after the answer itself.

6. Insert a brass brad into each hole.

7. Turn the folder over. Using 34-gauge crafting wire, wrap the end of the wire around the brad located near question one, and fold the prongs down to secure it.

8. Stretch the wire to the brad that corresponds to the current answer for question one. Wrap the wire around this brad and fold the prongs down to secure it. Cut off the remaining wire.

9. Cover the entire wire and two brads with masking tape.

10. Proceed with the next question in the same manner.

11. When all the questions have been properly wired, place the second press-board folder over the top of the first folder so that all the wires are covered. Staple it shut around the edges. (You may want to test the electro-board first before covering it by testing it with the continuity tester, as mentioned below.)

12. Using a continuity tester (available at any automotive store), the students should be able to choose the correct answer by resting the tester on the corresponding brad for each question. If the continuity tester lights up, the answer is correct (**Figure 2**).

Figure 2. An electro-board can help incorporate touch into an educational activity. (Source: Dr Karen Burke, from her reference paper, "Learning Style: The Clue to You!" Dr Burke can be reached at *KBurke105@msn.com*.)

Chapter 2

How Many Students Are Affected? What Does the Research Show?

One of the criticisms of the effectiveness of sensory-integration therapy is that it is not supported by enough research. Indeed, research in this area has been deficient over the years. Perhaps the most famous proponent of sensory-integration therapy was A. Jean Ayres. Ayres was an occupational therapist and psychologist who blended the two fields of science in her research. She published two books in the 1970s, entitled *Sensory Integration and Learning Disorders* (1972)[2] and *Sensory Integration and the Child* (1979).[3]

Ayres described the behavioral problems that are likely to occur when a child has inadequate sensory integration. She wrote, "Sensory integration theory proposes that sensory integration is a neurobiological process that organizes sensation from one's own body and from the environment and makes it possible to use the body effectively within the environment." Ayres felt that having knowledge of sensory integration was only one facet. Another was understanding how to apply this knowledge to change the behaviors of a student. Out of Ayres' research arose 17 standardized tests and many nonstandardized instruments to help identify and understand the multiple patterns of sensory-integration dysfunction. One of these, the Sensory Integration Praxis Test,[4] or SIPT, is considered the standard of reference for assessing sensory dysfunction. Ayres sought to remediate the disorder by using various techniques (thus coining the term *sensory-integration therapy*) to repeatedly expose the child to the offending sensory input within therapeutically designed activities to "normalize" his sensory systems.

Another researcher, B. M. Knickerbocker, proposed the theory that in some learning-disabled children, it was evident that their sensory dysfunction took on a form of sensory defensiveness. That is, the children were experiencing anxiety and problem behaviors due to their sensory-integration disorder. She proposed that some children were hyposensitive (underreactive) to sensory stimuli, while others were hypersensitive (overreactive) to such stimuli. Her book, *A Holistic Approach to the Treatment of Learning Disabilities* (1980),[5] added further clarification to the field of sensory disturbance and provided ways to address it.

First-person accounts of individuals who had SPD became prevalent in the 1990s. These included writings of Temple Grandin (*Emergence: Labeled Autistic,* 1996; and *Thinking in Pictures,* 1996),[6,7] Liane Holliday Willey (*Pretending to be Normal,* 1999), and Sean Barron (*There's a Boy in Here,* 1992).[8] These individuals described their attempts to deal with their sensory problems. Temple Grandin designed a "squeeze machine" to provide tactile input in the form of deep pressure. She wrote that this machine provided the deep pressure she needed to relieve stress. Some schools for special-needs children have duplicated her blueprint to build "squeeze machines" for use with children who have neurological disorders. Many claim that these machines have been useful and have resulted in a reduction of stress levels for some students. Ms Willey described how she frequently wore sunglasses indoors, owing to a heightened sense of vision and the overwhelming feeling of brightness that resulted. She also wrote about her problems with proprioception, as she navigated her way around a college campus and repeatedly got lost in buildings as she searched for her classroom. Mr Barron documents in his book how loud noises were very difficult for him to tolerate and contributed to problematic behaviors in school settings at times.

Ayres estimated that 5% to 10% of typically developing children experience sensory-integration problems to the extent that they could benefit from intervention. The prevalence of clinically significant SPD symptoms was 35% in one large study of 500 children from a gifted-and-talented center in a pilot study, and case studies of gifted children frequently mention unusually intense reactions to noise and pain.[9] These children frequently overreact to frustration. They may exhibit oversensitivity to textures, fluorescent lights, smells, and foods, as well as noise.[10]

> *Katie is an 8-year-old child who is gifted. Her mother describes her as "fussy" and particular about various things. One of the things that bothers Katie is handling chalk. When Katie is asked to go to the blackboard in math class, she frequently makes up an excuse about being allergic or ill so that she does not have to write on the board. Her teacher believes that Katie doesn't want to "show off" her math skills in front of the other students. When Katie finally confessed her problem with handling chalk, the school referred her for a psychological evaluation, when, in fact, Katie could have benefited from an occupational-therapy assessment.*

Stanley Greenspan and Serena Weider found that 94% of the children they evaluated with autism-spectrum disorders exhibited unusual sensory-processing patterns, with 39% described as underreactive, 19% as overreactive, and 36% as a mixture of both.[11] It has been reported that sensory dysfunction can be found in up to 70% of children who are labeled as "learning disabled" by their schools. Many children with Down syndrome have also been diagnosed with sensory dysfunction.

Dane is a toddler with Down syndrome. His mother actually enrolled him in a feeding program because of his unwillingness to eat certain foods, owing to their texture. Dane will independently eat no more than eight foods at 4 years of age and completely neglects foods that belong to the meat or vegetable food groups. This has resulted in a nutritional deficiency for Dane.

As we have seen, SPD is prevalent in our schools today. A child diagnosed with attention-deficit disorder, attention-deficit/hyperactivity disorder, or any form of an autism-spectrum disorder may also have sensory dysfunction. Children with learning disabilities (especially in reading, math, and handwriting) may demonstrate sensory dysfunction. A child diagnosed with dyspraxia (a deficit in motor movement) or central auditory-processing disorder (a deficit in the ability to process sounds, especially with background noise) may also be classified as a child with SPD.

Unfortunately, few students are evaluated or identified as having this problem by educators, and even fewer are receiving accommodations for this deficit in the classroom. What exactly is the reason for this lag in identification? Many schools do not recognize SPD as a disability that requires special-education services or accommodations. If the disorder is not identified by another label, such as one in the previous paragraph, then the child may not receive support.

SPD does not fit neatly into any of the categories that would make a child eligible for special-education services through an individualized education plan (IEP). Further, many schools would not even consider this disorder as one that would require accommodations through a 504 plan (a document prepared in accordance with the Americans with Disabilities Act, which allows children with disabilities who do not meet the criteria for special-education services to receive accommodations they need to be successful in their school settings). However, if a child qualifies for occupational therapy in school-based programs, this could be an avenue through which sensory-integration assistance could be obtained. It is helpful to show how the student needs sensory-integration components as part of his occupational-therapy program to be able to benefit from participation in the school curriculum or school day. If decisions are driven by data collection, sensory-integration techniques can then become required components in a child's IEP or 504. There is no language in the Individuals with Disabilities Education Act (the federal law comminly referred to as IDEA that governs the programs written for students with disabilities)[12] that prohibits the use of sensory integration within a classroom setting. The methodology used to address a particular child's problems is a team decision. Thus, an IEP team could decide to include sensory-integration components, whether or not the child has access to occupational therapy, if they felt it was appropriate.

Joshua was a 9-year-old boy with autism. He was deficient in the ability to regulate himself. Frequently, he flapped his hands, made mouth noises, and was off-task. On the basis of his parents' input, his teacher tried to provide a sensory diet for him at various times of the day. This consisted of exercises for him to do in his seat, an opportunity to take breaks, and stress-reduction toys he could manipulate at his desk. His teacher noticed a marked improvement in Joshua's ability to maintain attention to task and refrain from making mouth noises when this sensory diet was in place. Her anecdotal data clearly indicated an improvement in Joshua's behavior with the sensory diet. Nevertheless, the IEP team declared that Joshua's sensory program was not something that they had to provide according to IDEA, because Joshua did not qualify for occupational therapy. They refused to add these techniques to the IEP. Joshua's parents were worried that the teacher he would have next year might not be so cooperative with implementing the techniques. Joshua's parents could proceed to due process with the district and argue that their refusal to provide these accommodations was a violation of his right to receive specially designed instruction that was appropriate to his needs.

In this scenario, the parents would most likely win their case because of the data collection associated with Joshua's sensory-diet program. It is very unusual for a team to identify strategies that work for a particular student and then to later refuse to incorporate them in an IEP or 504. If the team had tried these strategies, and found through data collection that they did not work, Joshua's parents probably would not have had a case.

There have been some districts that have refused parental request for sensory-integration evaluations. This too, goes against the grain of IDEA. A child must be tested in all areas of his suspected disability. If the family "suspects" that SPD exists and requests that the district evaluate it, the district must comply or refer the family for a no-cost evaluation outside the district. Because SPD is so prevalent in children with learning disabilities and autism, a district would be remiss in not testing for this deficiency, as well.

Within IDEA, there is another category of eligibility that is sometimes used for children with SPD. It is referred to as Other Health Impaired, or OHI. According to IDEA, a child must have a disability that the district agrees with and also demonstrate a need for specially designed instruction. By using this category of eligibility, a district could then incorporate sensory accommodations into an IEP for a child whose degree of sensory impairment requires specially designed instruction.

Although there may not be enough research to support the idea that SPD can be remediated permanently, there are many anecdotal reports that sensory-integration techniques do help children and their families cope with SPD. In one case study conducted by David in 1990, a 24-year-old female was admitted to a psychiatric hospital for symptoms of anxiety (panic attacks) and depression.[13] The occupational therapist that evaluated her found that she had tactile, visual, and auditory defensiveness, as well as gravitational insecurity. She had learned to avoid certain situations and environments where she would be exposed to challenging stimuli. This learned avoidance response left her isolated socially, which contributed to her diagnosis of depression.

The occupational therapist that treated the young woman initiated a sensory diet to attempt to normalize her sensory system. A sensory diet consists of a variety of sensory techniques that are designed to expose the child, in a systematic and planned way, to sensory input. The belief is that repeated exposure in controlled ways will help normalize the child's responses. Being exposed to sensory items in a planned fashion helped the patient to realize that she could confront her sensory challenges in a proactive manner. This woman reported that she felt less threatened by sensory issues because she had also been provided with a plan that she could initiate to ward off panic attacks when she was exposed to the problem stimuli. This enabled her to function independently. While her sensory deficits were not remediated, she learned how to better cope with them so that they caused her less anxiety. As with any stressful situation, when one has an action plan to address anxiety, one no longer fears it. As a result, this particular young woman no longer avoided situations where exposure to unpleasant sensory stimuli would likely occur. Thus, the quality of her life improved greatly. Truly, sensory-integration therapy for older children and adults may take on a form of cognitive behavioral therapy, as well. Children must learn cognitive ways of coping with their disturbances to allow them to become active participants in society.

In one study by Ayres and Tickle in 1980, sensory-integration techniques were applied to children who displayed either hyperresponsive patterns to sensory stimuli or hyporesponsive (underresponsive) patterns.[14] The outcomes of the study converged with those of a study by Edelson et al (1999), which showed that applying deep pressure may help some children with hyperresponsiveness to such stimuli.[15] It should be noted, however, that in the Edelson research, physiological measurements acquired with galvanic skin tests showed that neither group of children benefited from such therapy. Could it be possible that frequent exposure to offensive sensory stimuli actually helped the children to learn to cope with it, although it didn't change their actual sensitivity to the offending stimuli?

In 1999, Stagnitti, Raison, and Ryan attempted to conduct research involving the effectiveness of a sensory diet with a 5-year-old boy with severe tactile defensiveness.[16] This child underwent a program of joint compression and skin brushing an average of three to five times daily for 2 weeks. There were also sensory activities implanted in his day between brushings that were designed to meet his sensory needs. Initially, his parents reported an increase in tolerance to tactile sensitivity. The brushing was then discontinued. However, after a period of regression, the therapy was reinitiated. The authors claimed that the child had been cured of his sensory defensiveness, but this claim was not supported by means of data collection. Further, other treatment modalities had been initiated during the course of the study, making it difficult to rule out the positive effects of these interventions as a reason for the improvement in his sensory processing.

In all of these cases, there were strong anecdotal reports that many subjects benefited in some way from sensory-integration therapy. Anecdotal reports are subjective—they contain the opinions and beliefs of subjects, family members, and the scientists who are conducting the studies. Looking at the data objectively, however, one would conclude that the data collection in these studies indicates that sensory-integration techniques were not useful for treating sensory disturbance. But let's continue on.

Because of the increase of foreign adoptions in the United States, adoptive families are becoming more aware of the role that sensory integration plays in healthy child development. There is a growing number of children who have been adopted that exhibit sensory disturbances and problem behaviors in their new lives. They may also be unable to form appropriate emotional bonds with their new adoptive families (sometimes referred to as *reactive attachment disorder*). Scientists believe that, as infants, these children may not have been able to develop the appropriate number of connections in the frontal cortexes of their brains because of a lack of exposure to sensory stimuli or because they were deprived of social interactions with their caregivers in the orphanages in which they lived. Some professionals believe that if adoptions occur before the age of 2 years, and children are adopted from orphanages where exposure to sensory stimuli and human contact are plentiful, these children will have fewer behavioral and emotional problems later on. So, the key may be that we must provide these interventions early in a child's life. Consider this study:

> *By using a single-subject research design, five preschool children with autism were examined to see if positive improvements could be demonstrated after the application of sensory-integration therapy techniques. Three behaviors were targeted, and samples of these behaviors were captured on videotape both before and after the intervention. The behaviors targeted*

*included nonengagement, goal-directed play,
and social interaction. A 3-week baseline period
was followed by one-on-one sessions with an
occupational therapist for 10 weeks. When the
baseline and intervention phases were compared,
four of the five children demonstrated a decrease
in the frequency of nonengaged behavior, three
demonstrated an increased frequency of goal-
directed play, and improvements were not noted
or were minimal for all five in the frequency of
their social interactions.*[17]

A child's brain develops essentially by creating new synapses and by the growth of dendrites (outgrowths from neurons that enable connections to happen) and axons (slender fibers that project from neuron to neuron). Sensory stimulation and experiences create more dendrites, which in turn produce more synapses. We can apply this knowledge to improve the way we design early-intervention programs for infants and toddlers, as well as for youngsters who have been adopted. If we include sensory-integration strategies in these programs for children who are very young, we may be able to create those pathways that would indeed lead to a cure for children with SPD. In other words, the earlier a child receives help for sensory problems, the better his outcome may be. If we know that children with particular disabilities are vulnerable to sensory disturbance (as an example, children with autism or infants with reactive attachment disorder), we can approach their treatments proactively, especially when they are identified at a younger age.

A child's brain must not only be able to modulate sensory input, it must also be able to inhibit it (stop it), habituate it (become accustomed to it), and facilitate it (allow him to act meaningfully and appropriately to it) if his corresponding behavior is to be appropriate.

Consider the simple sound of a child sharpening his pencil in the classroom. To downplay the noise so that it is not perceived as disruptive, our brains have to modulate the sound—turn it off or on, make it louder or softer—as we need it to. My brain might "turn it on" when I realize that I, too, need to sharpen my pencil. It might "turn it on" when I notice that Johnny was allowed to get up and sharpen his pencil, so I must be able to sharpen mine, too. I have thus used the sound to facilitate my behavior. If I hadn't heard the sound of the sharpener, I may never have decided I needed to sharpen my own pencil. If I am trying to finish a math paper, however, I might say to myself, "Oh, that's the pencil sharpener," and disregard the sound. In this case, I have *habituated* the sound of the sharpener—I know what it sounds like, so I don't have to look up or even attend to it. When I disregard the sound, I am inhibiting it from interfering with my work. Brains that can inhibit, habituate, and facilitate sensory input appropriately will most likely result in individuals who can attend, stay on task, and complete work. Brains that do not process sensory input correctly have problems in three areas: They don't receive messages, they receive messages inconsistently, or they connect improperly with other sensory messages. No part of the nervous system works alone: "Touch aids vision, vision aids balance, balance aids body awareness, and movement aids learning."[18]

If it is difficult or not possible to *remediate* a child's disability, then what remains for us to do is help the child and school learn to *accommodate* it. Making accommodations is a way to provide relief to children who experience the assaults of a sensory system that is not working properly, affecting their lives academically, emotionally, physically, and socially. If accommodations help to alleviate some of the problematic behaviors associated with SPD, then it's important to be open minded about how sensory-integration techniques could be useful in the classroom.

The other piece that would be important to include in educational programs is stress management. Children with sensory dysfunction often experience tremendous stress, and attempts to cope with a bombardment of sensory stimuli may be exhausting. In addition, oftentimes children can better cope with sensory stimuli *when they expect it,* as opposed to *when it takes them by surprise.*

> *Elizabeth had difficulty with auditory sensitivity. On her first day of school, she could not sit in the cafeteria without covering her ears. She cried almost the entire lunch period and refused to eat. For the rest of the afternoon, she was jumpy and exhibited self-stimulatory behaviors. Elizabeth's team had neglected to prepare her for the noises in the cafeteria. Had Elizabeth been provided with a visual schedule of her day and learned just how long lunch was and what would come next, she may have been better able to cope with it.*

For this reason, it is vital that parents be active participants in meetings with their child's school administrators and teachers, so that they can inform them of possible problematic times of the day. Only parents or caregivers or previous staff members who have worked with the child may be able to provide this type of information. The more we can prepare ahead of time for children with sensory disturbance, the more likely these children will experience success. Planning ahead also allows us to provide kids with opportunities to learn stress-management techniques.

> *Angelo had difficulty with auditory sensitivity. Angelo's parents informed his teachers and staff members that he would most likely fall apart if he were exposed to a fire-drill bell. Angelo's mother explained that if Angelo was prepared for the drill, or even knew when to anticipate it, he may respond appropriately. After a discussion about how the school could accommodate this*

problem, the principal decided that he would bring Angelo to the office and let him activate the system while wearing headphones. The plan was a success. In addition, Angelo learned that he could indeed cope with the drill if he knew it was about to happen.

Because parents and caregivers can often provide the most information about their child's sensory-processing abilities, the Sensory Profile Caregiver Questionnaire has been developed as part of an entire assessment, called *The Sensory Profile.* It was authored by Winnie Dunn in 1999 and is available through Therapy Skill Builders in San Antonio, Texas.[19]

Reader Questions

1. **I am confused! So, can we cure SPD or not?**
   Unfortunately, this is not entirely conclusive, though what has been discovered through research is that a cure is unlikely. Children who are provided with intensive therapy before the age of 5 years are the most likely ones to benefit from any form of early intervention. These children may indeed have some of their symptoms remediated. What we do know is that sensory-integration techniques can provide relief to some children...indeed, they can help them become more attentive and productive in their home, school, and community settings. Further, we also know that sensory-integration methods can help to normalize how an individual feels about these disturbances, to the point where they can function better in settings where the offending stimuli is present.

2. **How long should I implement sensory-integration therapy for my child?** *This is a decision based entirely on your own child's progress with sensory-integration therapy. If, through data collection, you and your child's therapist continue to see progress in normalizing his responses to offensive stimuli, then by all means, keep the program going!*

3. Are all occupational therapists trained in sensory-integration, or SI, therapy?

Many occupational therapists have been exposed to sensory-integration therapy, but it is important to ask how many courses they have taken or how many direct contact hours they have had with this type of therapy. In addition, sensory-integration therapy is not limited to just occupational therapists. Speech therapists and behavioral specialists may also have experience using this methodology.

Chapter 3
Data-Driven Decisions

When a child exhibits behavioral problems that affect his learning or the learning of others, the school team should consider a functional behavioral assessment. Functional behavioral assessments are designed to discover what is causing the problem behavior (ie, the function). When data drives decisions, behavioral plans are likely to be more effective.

> *Rachel was an 8-year-old student with Asperger syndrome. She had a long history of problem behavior associated with auditory and tactile stimuli. If the classroom was too noisy, or if there were unexpected noises (fire alarms, chairs scraping the floor, buzzers), Rachel would often cover her ears and begin crying and screaming. It was obvious that such noises were painful to her. She also exhibited problems with her sense of touch. Frequently, it was impossible to touch her in any way, and her reactions were often aggressive when she was touched unexpectedly. A simple encouraging pat on the back would often send her into a violent episode. Her mother reported that, at times, Rachel would refuse to wear certain fabrics, such as corduroy or denim, and often preferred to wear shorts instead of long pants.*

If Rachel's school team were to record data about her episodes, it would be important to decide what method of data collection would be most effective. In Rachel's case, her behaviors are *discrete:* There is a clear beginning and end to each tantrum. Each behavior is observable and measurable. Because Rachel's team is concerned about how many of these behaviors she is exhibiting and if this number can be reduced, it would seem useful to collect this type of data as a frequency count. If we record this data for 2 consecutive weeks, we can not only get an idea of how many behaviors are occurring in any given week, but also see if there is a trend developing (for example, is the number of problem behaviors increasing or decreasing?).

If we number the left side of a piece of paper in column format, in consecutive order from the bottom of the paper to the top, we can tally the number of total behavioral episodes each day for 2 weeks (see the following diagram). If we "connect the dots," we can create a line graph that pertains specifically to Rachel. This enables us to determine, at a glance, how many of these behaviors Rachel is demonstrating, and also if there is a trend in the number (increase or decrease) of these behaviors.

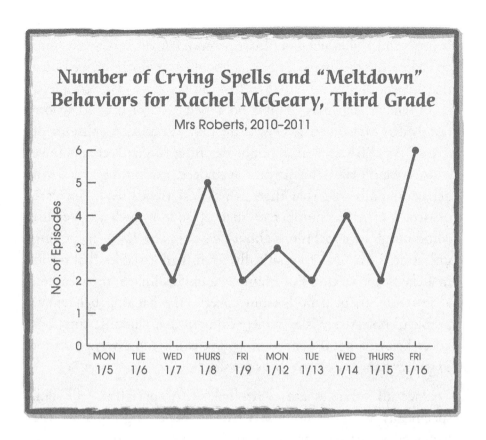

Number of Crying Spells and "Meltdown" Behaviors for Rachel McGeary, Third Grade

Mrs Roberts, 2010–2011

Clearly, Rachel is having a substantial number of crying spells and meltdown behaviors. What is not clear is if these behaviors are related to sensory dysfunction. What is also uncertain is whether or not Rachel is showing an increase or decrease in such behaviors over time. For some children, 2 weeks' worth of data collection may not be enough to establish a trend. If the child has been sick, for instance, poor behavior may result from his physical condition. Or, the particular week we decide to record data may also be of concern. The week before a holiday break, as an example, may be a time when many children exhibit problematic behaviors.

Applied behavioral analysis (ABA) is the field of study in which behavior is examined and measured—that is, behaviors are observed and counted. ABA seeks to filter out all competing variables (such as a child being sick or the problems associated with the week before vacation), so that data that is analyzed is pure and unbiased. For this reason, ABA does not take into consideration the internal states of its subjects. However, we know that internal states do have an effect on behavior (for example, a child who is sick may exhibit poor behavior, or a child whose family has welcomed a new baby may experience episodes of stress). An ABA specialist might examine the data chart above and conclude that the student is indeed exhibiting meltdown behaviors daily and that there is no clear trend (ie, an increase or decrease in the number of such episodes). Such a specialist could not draw conclusions about *why* the behavior is happening unless he/she could systematically control all variables that occur in a classroom setting (for example, a child's illness, the weather, a new teacher, or a bothersome peer). Approaching behavioral problems objectively is extremely difficult in a school setting, but nevertheless, a good behavioral specialist should always attempt to gather data as objectively as possible.

Once all variables are controlled, ABA specialists will look specifically at the stimulus (what happened right before the behavior occurred) that triggered the behavior. If the reaction to the stimulus can be observed, it can be counted. Unfortunately, we cannot always observe how a student feels when he is becoming overwhelmed with sensory stimuli. If the classroom gets too noisy and he covers his ears, we can formulate an educated guess that the sound may be too loud for him. If he spills water on his clothes and then becomes agitated, we may surmise that his wet clothes are irritating him. However, these are only educated guesses. As an example, a child may cover his ears not because the noises around him are bothersome, but because he may have an ear infection!

ABA specialists frequently describe the function of any given student's behavior as "escape" or "attention." This means that the student is using his behavior to get out of doing something or to gain attention from his peers or his teacher. In school settings, we then have to consider what the child may be attempting to "escape" from (a certain academic subject, certain peers, a particular module of the student's day, or sensory stimuli) and why these episodes are increasing in frequency. ABA also tells us that the frequency of behaviors tends to increase when the behaviors are being reinforced (rewarded).

Charles had substantial difficulty with math. Frequently, when presented with math work to do, he would get agitated and flap his hands. Despite his teacher's attempts to help him remain calm, Charles would inevitably cry, scream, or throw objects. Because these behaviors were distracting and sometimes dangerous to the other students, his teacher would remove him from the classroom. When data was collected and analyzed with regard to the frequency of these negative behaviors in math class, Charles displayed an increase in not only the frequency of his behaviors, but also in how quickly he initiated these behaviors. Additionally, instead of only occurring in math class, now they were occurring in other modules, as well. Charles was clearly attempting to escape from doing his work, and his behavior was being reinforced by his teacher each time she removed him from the classroom.

Matthew exhibited defiant behaviors at school. If he did not want to do his work, his defiance quickly escalated, and he demonstrated a series of aggressive actions (throwing the materials, hitting the peers next to him, or striking out at the adults around him). Matthew was placed on a half-day schedule because his behaviors were so violent. Whenever he initiated aggression, his parents were called, and he was removed from school. When a behavioral specialist tracked the data, it was found that not only had the number of Matthew's aggressive acts increased, but he was also initiating them much sooner in the day. Being sent home was the reinforcer, and he quickly learned that if he hit or kicked, he could get there faster. To turn this scenario around, it became necessary for Matthew's school team to make school more reinforcing than going home. Matthew was given small increments of work that he enjoyed and was reinforced frequently with computer time (something he loved!) if he completed them. Gradually, more meaningful work was introduced, and the period until the delivery of reinforcement was extended so that the reinforcement occurred less frequently. It is important to note, however, that Matthew was not being provided with academic work at his ability level early on, and his sensory disturbances were also not taken into consideration. His new behavioral plan provided specific accommodations for these issues, as well.

As mentioned previously, we must also consider the word "escape" when it comes to sensory-based behaviors. Even though we cannot know the internal states of our subjects, we can collect the data that measures the result of these internal states. As we discussed earlier, many children will attempt to escape from sensory input that is disturbing to them. By "tweaking" Rachel's data-collection chart from earlier, we may be able to discover if any of her behaviors may actually be related to sensory disturbances.

It would be important to take into consideration any anecdotal data that could accompany the graph. Anecdotal data is report-type data. For instance, the teacher (Mrs Roberts) could add to the information provided to us in the previous chart by describing what the student was doing during this period of time. She could tell us what subject was being taught or in what location the behaviors occurred. She could also describe the topography of the behavior (how the behavior looked). An example of topography would be the following:

> *Rachel covered her ears and cried when the tag game was initiated in physical-education class. She hunched her shoulders together to avoid being touched. The kids were screaming and chasing each other, and it was very chaotic.*

Whatever information Rachel's teacher can give us about her behaviors, either orally or in writing, is also part of data collection and can be very valuable. Here is an example of anecdotal information provided by Mrs Roberts for January 11:

> *Rachel had three incidences of crying today. In the first incident, the students had a morning assembly in the auditorium. This assembly consisted of a nature film, with music playing in the background. As soon as the film began to play, Rachel covered her ears and began to cry. I felt the volume was rather high, myself. The next incident occurred during a written-expression assignment. Rachel became extremely frustrated as she tried to think of a topic and begin the assignment. She started to cry, and I allowed her to take a walk and get a drink. The third incident came at lunchtime in the cafeteria. Someone bumped into her in line, and she turned around and hit the child behind her. When I told her to apologize and explained that the child had not hit her on purpose, she started to cry.*

In addition, Mrs Roberts was asked to write about any other times that she has observed Rachel crying. Here is what she wrote:

> *Rachel sometimes cries when things are too hard for her academically. During these times, I have observed her hitting her head with her hand and becoming increasingly agitated.*

Many times, in school settings, anecdotal information is collected with regard to problem behaviors, but it is rarely analyzed for true meaning. Thus, collecting data for the sake of collecting data is meaningless. Because of a plethora of required paperwork, teachers have little time during the day for this type of data collection if it is not going to be utilized and supported by quantitative data. Many times, this type of data is going to be brief, and it may not give us all that we need. For this reason, anecdotal data should *supplement, and not replace* objective data. Further, anecdotal data is often *subjective* data. This data may contain the writer's opinions and feelings. For instance, in the sample above, Mrs Roberts writes:

> *"...I felt the volume was rather high, myself."*

Mrs Roberts is leading the reader to conclude that the volume of the film was too high, and thus Rachel found it difficult to handle, covered her ears, and began to cry. But, Rachel also may have covered her ears and cried because the students around her were singing and whistling to the music. The singing and whistling, coupled with the volume of the film, produced a cacophony of sound that may have put Rachel into a state of overload. If we were going to use Mrs Roberts' anecdotal reporting and her opinions to decide future interventions for Rachel, it may be concluded that Rachel should not participate in school assemblies. But that conclusion would not be appropriate! Rachel will not learn to tolerate such situations if she is allowed to escape them. Indeed, allowing her to do this may create an avoidance pattern with other social aspects of school. Thus, the team must look for accommodations to help her remain with her peers. If Rachel had a set of earplugs that she could insert when auditory stimuli became too much for her, she may well indeed be able to participate in assemblies at her school. Thus, a disability (ie, SPD) that may not be remediated (according to current research) could certainly be *accommodated*.

Let's assume that we used anecdotal reporting to supplement our objective data collection. We could create a "legend" of letters to help us incorporate Mrs Roberts' data into our own objective data:

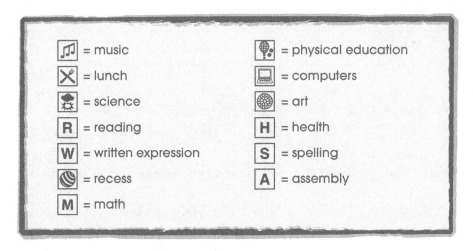

By using Mrs Roberts' same graph, this is additional information we can learn about Rachel's behaviors:

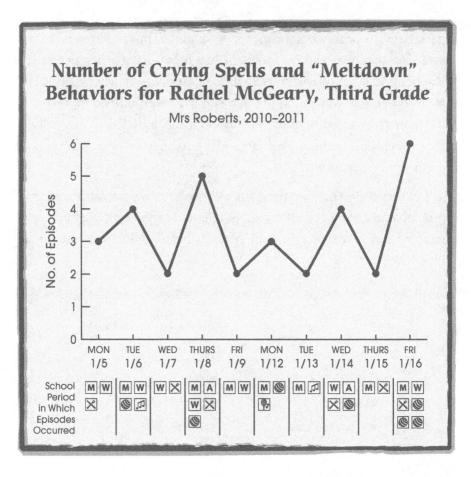

Number of Crying Spells and "Meltdown" Behaviors for Rachel McGeary, Third Grade

Mrs Roberts, 2010–2011

Conclusions: Over a span of 10 days, the student had problems six times during lunch, seven times during recess (on one day she had three episodes of crying during recess), one time during physical education, two times during music, eight times during math, seven times during written expression, and two times during an assembly. We now know that she needs additional supports in lunch, recess, physical-education class, music class, math, written expression, and assemblies. With the above information, combined with Mrs Roberts' description of the topography of the incidents, we may be able to successfully conclude that there are sensory problems occurring in at least five modules of Rachel's day (lunch, recess, physical education, music, and assembly) and that there might also be concerns about the appropriateness of accommodations/adaptations provided to her in math and written expression.

What about children who exhibit problematic behaviors that do not have a clear beginning or end, making it extremely difficult to count them? Or, how do we measure behaviors that occur with such frequency that it is nearly impossible to keep track of them? An example would be a case of self-stimulatory behavior—that is, behavior that an individual uses to repeatedly stimulate him- or herself.

> *Sarah engages in frequent self-stimulatory behaviors. She flaps her hands frequently. She may begin flapping for a period of time, stop briefly, and then start again. She may also flick her fingers in front of her eyes. It is difficult to even get a frequency count, as the behavior appears to go on and on. It seems to happen in all modules of the child's day, with no rhyme or reason as to its beginning or end.*

When children exhibit behaviors similar to Sarah's, we may need to create an interval-recording data-collection tool. An interval-recording tool enables us to record the behavior as it occurs across various time slots during a school day—in other words, we measure it within specified time intervals. The interval length can be whatever time period can be devoted to collecting data, but there should be sufficient intervals to capture the behavior. The data recorded should also be random—we don't want to avoid certain time periods if we are going to be able to make objective decisions about what the data shows. For instance, if the behavioral specialist decides not to record data in music class because she has a prior obligation during that time, then she may be leaving out a valuable time period that is frequently an area of concern with regard to children who have sensory disturbance.

Interval-Recording Chart
for Sarah Jones, Fourth Grade
Mr Ryan, 2010–2011

Observation Interval	MON 10/5	TUES 10/6	WED 10/7	THURS 10/8	FRI 10/9
8:15–8:30	✓	✓	✓	✓	✓
9:45–10:00		✓	✓	✓	✓
11:15–11:30	✓	✓		✓	✓
12:15–12:30	✓	✓	✓	✓	✓
1:00–1:15	✓		✓		
2:30–2:45	✓	✓	✓	✓	
3:15–3:30	✓	✓	✓	✓	✓

Conclusions: This data-collection chart for Sarah shows that she is indeed demonstrating a great deal of self-stimulatory behavior throughout the day. If we incorporate her academic subjects into the chart, we can see not only the times of the day that are giving Sarah problems, but also what is happening during those times:

Observation Interval	School Period	MON 10/5	TUES 10/6	WED 10/7	THURS 10/8	FRI 10/9
8:15–8:30	Arrival	✓	✓	✓	✓	✓
9:45–10:00	Reading		✓	✓	✓	✓
11:15–11:30	Lunch	✓	✓		✓	✓
12:15–12:30	Recess	✓	✓	✓	✓	✓
1:00–1:15	Music M/W, Art T/Th, Computers Fri	✓		✓		
2:30–2:45	Social Studies	✓	✓	✓	✓	
3:15–3:30	Dismissal	✓	✓	✓	✓	✓

Once the team decides what interventions would be appropriate for Sarah, we should then do another interval sampling to see if those interventions are working. If they are, fewer occurrences should be noted on the interval-sampling chart.

Many occupational therapists are recommending a sensory diet for children with sensory disturbances in school settings. The assumption is that children with sensory dysfunction may need additional planned sensory experiences to help normalize their systems. Sensory diets are often recommended for children who exhibit sensory dysfunction and may include a variety of sensory experiences, consisting of (but not limited to) manipulation of stress-reduction toys; use of mints or other gustatory input; use of inflatable seat cushions, beanbag chairs, rocking chairs, isometric exercises, trampolines, and weighted vests or lap pads; and also time spent outside of the classroom to provide additional input.

Certain items included in any recommended diet may be intrusive in the classroom and could possibly disturb other children. In addition, some of the items are not easily portable.

If they work for the child in one part of the school day, it makes sense to have another set of the same interventions for other locations where he may be during school hours. For instance, if the child leaves one classroom for another, he should have these same interventions available to him in the next classroom (such as going from a regular-education classroom to a learning-support classroom). After all, a child's disability is not contained in just one classroom! For these reasons, we want to be sure that the sensory-diet items are truly working for the student. The only way to ensure this is by incorporating a systematic period of data collection for each item on the sensory diet and by initiating each in isolation of the other.

As an educational consultant for children with special needs, it is frustrating to enter a classroom and see a variety of sensory-diet items scattered around a child's desk. Many times these items fall on the floor, break, become lost, or are used in inappropriate ways by the student, as well as by his peers. Thus, instead of becoming useful items to improve the student's productivity, they become distractions. Rarely is each item's effectiveness measured by means of objective data acquisition. Frequently, the teacher expresses mixed opinions about whether the items are useful at all. *We must use data to determine if interventions are effective before they become part of a student's intervention plan. Otherwise, what we thought would be useful may end up causing more problematic behaviors.*

If we examine Sarah's chart, we note that after she has arrived at school, she exhibits many self-stimulatory behaviors. If we formulate a hypothesis and assume that the sensory disturbances of the bus and the explosion of sensory stimuli that occurs as she enters the classroom may be causing this, it might make sense for us to try providing her with a sensory "downtime" right before she begins her reading module. Her team decided to remove Sarah from morning activities and give her a few moments of sensory deprivation in a quiet area of the classroom under a table covered with a long tablecloth. Sarah could sit on a beanbag chair under the table and listen to quiet nature sounds while wearing headphones and looking at a favorite book. The team decided to verify their hypothesis with data collection, as depicted in the following chart.

Observation Interval	School Period	MON 11/3	TUES 11/4	WED 11/5	THURS 11/6	FRI 11/7
8:15–8:30	Arrival	✓	✓	✓	✓	✓
9:45–10:00	Reading	✓				

After the team arranged for Sarah to have some sensory "downtime" before beginning her first module, Sarah experienced a reduction in self-stimulatory behaviors during reading. As a bonus, the team noted that she was more attentive and less fidgety during this time period. Because they had such remarkable success with the sensory-intervention techniques with Sarah, they decided to give them a try again before her social studies module. Lunch, recess, and music were also times of the day that provided too much sensory input for her. Her team looked for ways to provide some support during these times. She was encouraged to use her headphones and choose a place to sit that was less stimulating during lunch and music, and a visual schedule was provided for her in music. In this way, she could learn to anticipate what activities would be challenging for her in the music module, prepare herself for them, and self-advocate by telling her teacher if it was too much stimuli.

It should be noted that Sarah's team should not permit Sarah to wear her headphones for the entire day. Doing so may cause Sarah to use them to escape all auditory input, with the end result that her hearing may become even more sensitive.

By means of data collection, the outcome of this planning revealed that in her social studies module, there was a reduction in self-stimulatory behavior. For Sarah, these interventions should be written in the "Specially Designed Instruction" section of her IEP. Not only did her team feel *(subjectively)* that the interventions were useful, but because they were backed up by *(objective)* data, they served as "best practice" for Sarah.

Reader Questions

1. **Wow! Are all these data collections really necessary? I am a teacher and I just don't have time to do all of this!** *Understandably, you are most likely a busy person. But, with any given behavior, if you don't understand what's driving it, you most likely won't be able to address it in an appropriate way. You could spend just as much time writing a behavioral plan that doesn't work only to have to throw it away. It's always best to make decisions based on data.*

2. **I thought my anecdotal data was useful! Are you saying that it isn't?** *Of course not! Any good behavioral specialist will ask you for your input. It's only when we rely solely on anecdotal input that we lose the validity of data collection. Everyone has a personal opinion about why problem behaviors happen. The key word, however, is "personal." Personal opinions are oftentimes not supported by facts.*

3. **I have some sensory-diet items that I use for a particular student with SPD. Would they work for another student?** *They may, or they may not. Just as you selected items through data collection that worked for your first student, you should also be systematic with selecting items for your*

*second student. If the data supports
the hypothesis that they are useful for
this second student, then, by all means,
implement them for her, as well!*

Chapter 4
Signs and Symptoms of SPD

Often, recognizing sensory dysfunction in students is fairly easy. For instance, a student who covers his ears is obviously experiencing a problem with his auditory sense. A student who refuses to eat a certain food may be deficient in his gustatory-processing ability. A student who doesn't like to be touched or refuses to wear certain fabrics may have tactile defensiveness. We refer to these children as being hypersensitive to certain sensory stimuli. They may become vigilant about attempting to escape situations that bother them. The author affectionately refers to them as "sensory hightailers," because of their tendency to "hightail it" out of the situation that disturbs them. They are our *sensory avoiders*.

> *One parent reports that his son Sam, as a youngster, was the only child he ever saw who didn't enjoy having people sing "Happy Birthday" to him. Sam would cover his ears and wait anxiously for the song to end.*

Just as frequently, however, we may discover children who have additional difficulties. Consider the child who doesn't seem to feel pain. He is rough with other kids and craves big hugs, and his parents report that he likes to squeeze between the sofa cushions to nap. He seems to have no awareness of food around his mouth when he eats his lunch. This student may not be getting enough sensory input to his tactile system. Or you may notice a student in your classroom who frequently smells materials. He may be attempting to "rev up" his olfactory sense. We refer to these children as being hyposensitive. On the flip side, some hyposensitive children appear withdrawn, tired, and underaroused, or they have a low energy level. Because of their inability to rev themselves up, these same children may use self-stimulatory behavior (tapping pencils, wiggling feet, playing with hair, flicking fingers, flapping hands) to gain the input that they are not getting normally. Hyposensitive children may have poor muscle tone. They may have difficulty holding their carriage up, their abdominal muscles are often weak, and they prefer sedentary types of activities. Many hyposensitive children are *sensory seekers.* They tend to look for ways to compensate for their underreactive sensory systems by seeking out experiences that will provide them with sensory input.

To further complicate matters, imagine being an individual who seems to process sensory input efficiently in one situation, but then has great difficulty in another area. Some individuals report that their auditory sense appears to function in a similar way to the volume knob on a radio—sometimes the volume is too high, and at other times, it is too low.

> *Ian is a 17-year-old boy who loves to attend rock concerts. He dances, sings along, and seems to have no difficulty participating alongside other teens in this loud, noisy, chaotic environment. However, Ian refuses to attend pep rallies at school. He says that the noise in the gym puts him in sensory overload. Anyone who witnesses his attempts to participate in such an environment will observe that he becomes irritated and restless. Ian says the acoustics, smells, and confined seating in the gym are sensory input that, when combined, create an intolerable situation for him.*

Or, consider Ryan:

> *Ryan is an 18-year-old boy who has no difficulty with individuals who wear perfume or scented lotions. However, if he is attending church service for an hour and is seated in a packed pew, he will immediately notice the smells that can accompany this social situation: bad breath, lack of deodorant, heavy perfumes, and lingering cigarette smoke. He reports that these smells are so overwhelming that he can't concentrate on what is going on around him. His realization that the service is only an hour and his sheer will to remain calm are the only things that get him through the service without having an episode.*

There are children who lack the ability to filter out sensory stimuli. The filtering process has a direct effect on their behavioral-inhibition mechanism. For instance, let's say a student is working diligently on his math homework, when another student gets up to sharpen his pencil or throw something away, or he calls out to get attention. Most students will be able to inhibit these sounds and remain on task. They can disregard the sounds, thus preventing them from interfering with their current level of focus. However, a child who lacks the ability to filter sounds will hear every noise at the same volume. He will not be able to attend well to tasks when the room is noisy. Thus, he will appear to have problems with behavioral inhibition. He will not be able to inhibit the noise and will allow it to interfere with his work. As his teacher, you will see him off-task and will probably urge him to focus on the work at hand. Truly, however, he is not attempting to escape his work; rather, he is having difficulty processing sensory input efficiently. To accommodate his disability, you might implement a different method of classroom management. For instance, you might ask children not to leave their seats in the middle of tasks or request that they raise their hand to get your assistance, instead of calling out.

There are also children who are learning to tolerate their sensory differences, but have problems when there are no considerations or accommodations made for their disability.

> *Mary, a 13-year-old girl with sensory dysfunction, appears to be able to handle her sensory challenges fairly well. Although things are noisy at times, she covers her ears and proceeds to do whatever it is that is expected of her, without incident. The more of these sensory challenges she is confronted with, the more irritated she becomes. Sometimes her teachers can see by the end of the day that her irritability is definitely increasing. Often, she complains of being tired. However, she has never exhibited meltdown behaviors during school. After school, it's a different story. Her family reports that she flies into violent rages immediately after stepping off the bus. It may be that the loud bus is the last sensory straw for Mary. Or, it may be that home is her safe spot, the place where she can vent.*

Or, consider the case of Aaron:

> *Aaron is a 7-year-old boy. His parents report that he enjoys swimming and taking baths. He has no problems with getting his face and hair wet. However, if his clothes get wet, he will scream and cry until he is provided with dry clothes.*

Or, finally, there's Alex:

> *Alex is a 5-year-old boy. He will eat brussels sprouts, liver, and spinach—foods that many*

other children his age will avoid. However, he refuses to eat potato chips, Doritos, and Fritos. He says he can't stand the crunching sound they make.

When we consider that efficient processing of sensory stimuli results in effective arousal levels, individuals who have normal sensory-processing abilities will often be the same folks who will be able to maintain attention to task, control their impulses, tolerate frustration, balance their emotions, and demonstrate efficient motor ability.[20] Children who cannot do these things may be children with sensory dysfunction.

We haven't yet discussed the vestibular (balance) or proprioceptive (awareness of where our body is in space) senses. These two often go unrecognized in a school setting, but here are some examples of how difficulties with them might manifest. If you see any of the following, you might have a child who has difficulties with these senses:

- A child who seems hesitant about using stairs
- A child who lacks coordination ability in physical-education class or at other times of the day
- A child who has difficulty copying or coordinating motor movements to songs or games (eg, "Simon Says," "Head and Shoulders")
- A child who has difficulty distinguishing left from right
- A child who avoids playground equipment or who can't tear himself away from it
- A child who has difficulty climbing up or going down bleachers
- A child who has no awareness of personal space when speaking to others, or who frequently seems to be "all over everyone" during carpet or circle time

- A child who frequently trips or falls

- A child who can't sit in his seat, falls out, sits on his foot, sits on the edge, "perches" with his bottom off the floor, or simply prefers to stand while he works

- A child who frequently wiggles or uses excessive amounts of self-stimulatory behavior

- A child who can't time his body movements to get on an escalator

- A child who gets "lost" in the hallway or can't find his room

- A child who feels unbalanced when asked to walk on carpets containing patterns that skew his depth perception or to step from a carpet onto a hard floor

- A child that refuses to jump off a low-built wall or steps because they appear much higher to him than they actually are

- A child who can't stand on one foot

- A child who becomes nauseated or dizzy when his head is moved

- A child who is unaware when his or her center of gravity has changed; for instance, when stepping down from a curb or onto uneven flooring

- A child who appears to be sleepy or have a low energy level most of the time

- A child who appears to be "wound up" or hyperactive

- A child with a poor self-concept ("I hate P.E.! I stink at sports!")

- A child who walks on his toes

- A child with a wide stance

- A child who turns his whole body to look at a person or object

As we can see with these manifestations, our vestibular and proprioceptive senses can certainly affect the way we perform during our school day.

Joseph was deficient in his ability to process proprioceptive and tactile input, and he also lacked a sense of balance. Physical-education activities were often a disaster for him. He could not catch or throw very well, he had an awkward gait, and activities like jumping rope, using a Hula-hoop, and hopping were extremely difficult for him to imitate, even with peers or teachers demonstrating the movements. During the last 10 minutes of the school day, his teacher would line the students up in anticipation of the arrival of the bus. Joseph frequently took the last spot in line to avoid being touched by his peers. One day, an overhead projector was left on the floor behind where Joseph was standing. One of the children initiated a gentle push from the front of the line, causing Joseph to lose his balance and topple backwards into the machine, shattering its glass top. His teacher reprimanded him for not being more careful. Joseph was distraught, as he felt responsible for the accident. Clearly, his sensory deficits were affecting the course of his school day, and the accident was not his fault.

Consider this preschool child's story:

Sam was a 5-year-old boy in preschool. During circle time, the children would sit "criss-cross applesauce"-style on their individual carpet mats. Frequently, half of Sam's body would be on the carpet and the other half on the floor. He would stretch out his legs and lean back into other students' personal space. He had great difficulty managing his own body orientation when compared with others.

Or this child's tale:

Allison struggled with handwriting. Often, she pushed down so hard on the pencil that the lead snapped off. Although she could write her letters neatly, she could rarely finish a writing assignment without incident. Breaking the lead on the pencil and taking longer than others to finish her assignments frustrated her. The occupational therapist explained to the teacher that the problem was not her handwriting, it was her sensory system—specifically, the proprioceptive and tactile senses. Allison could not feel the pressure she was exerting on the pencil. What she believed was an appropriate sense of touch on the pencil was really too hard.

In a school setting, we may not be aware of gustatory difficulties that some children may have. If we have a chance to observe their eating habits in the cafeteria, we may notice some sensory challenges in this setting, as well. There are children whose parents must pack their lunch each day. If they don't, they know that their kids may not eat. Some children would rather go hungry than eat a food with a texture that is revolting to them. For this reason, they may refuse to eat foods such as pudding, tapioca, or yogurt. For others, it's not the texture they can't tolerate; it's the taste. These particular students may only eat a limited variety of foods (chicken fingers, noodles without sauce, hot dogs, or macaroni and cheese).

There are other children who can't stand the sound the foods make when they chew. They may hum while eating them to provide themselves with a form of distraction.

For many families with a child who has SPD, the process of sitting down together and eating a meal is likened to entering a war zone. Arguing with the child, punishing him, force-feeding, and using bribes may all be undertaken in an effort to make him eat. Teachers and administrators need to realize that many children will go into the latter half of their afternoon calorie-starved because they have not eaten their lunch (and for some, their breakfast, as well). This problem must be distinguished from mere "fussiness." Fussy children will generally find something to nibble on and may succumb to peer pressure. Children with genuine SPD frequently do not improve their eating habits in environments outside the family home. They often lack an adequate intake of nutrients, which leads to vitamin and mineral deficiencies. Frequently, the only way to address these disturbances is by using a behavioral approach.

When trying to get a child to eat, we want him or her to associate good things with the food. We may start with an offending food and have the child play with it. For instance, he may use pudding to finger-paint, or he may use vegetables to create a fort. If he can do these things, he will earn a preferred reinforcer (reward). The reinforcer has to be powerful. Often it is helpful to survey the student or parents to discover what toys or activities he finds enjoyable. These are usually excellent reinforcers.

The next step in the chain may be for him to hold the offensive food to his cheek. Then, in another session, he may be asked to kiss it. He may then be asked to hold it to his lips. Next, he may be asked to lick it once. Gradually, each discrete step in the process of eating the offending food, and pairing success with reinforcement, will yield the end result of the child being able to put the food in his mouth, chew it, and swallow it. After multiple successes with eating one particular food type, the food is then generalized into his diet.

At this point, it needs to be noted that children with sensory disturbances have learned to tolerate these foods, but they still may not prefer them. Thus, if parents allow the child to select his food choices, or avoid those foods again, they will inadvertently reinforce escape. This will certainly result in a regression of his behavior, as he will most likely not choose the offensive foods.

Although addressing food intolerances may not seem to fall within the jurisdiction of most typical school settings, teachers and administrators should be aware of how gustatory disturbances can affect a student's functioning level, as well as his ability to be attentive and actively engaged in the learning process. If a student is calorie deprived, it will certainly be difficult to maintain ultimate attention levels. Some children may go through their whole day without eating enough food to enable them to be active learners. They may develop headaches, have dizzy spells, or become dehydrated from the lack of fluids that they would normally get from regular food intake. They may experience low blood sugar and become confused, emotional, or even volatile. What may seem like a problem that should be dealt with at home can certainly spill over and become a school concern, as well.

Another sensory disturbance that is often overlooked in the classroom involves the way a child processes visual input. In today's schools, it has become a tradition for teachers to decorate or cover just about every square inch of their classroom walls with artwork, instructional phrases, motivational posters, and the like. Oftentimes, there are mobiles or student crafts hanging from the ceiling. Although this visual stimuli makes the classroom look busy and productive to an outside observer, it may serve as visual "clutter" for a student who has trouble processing this type of stimuli. There are also children whose visual acuity is so predominant that they can see the flicker of fluorescent lights.

This type of environment may be overstimulating for certain types of students. Such children may benefit from being allowed to wear sunglasses indoors and from a seating assignment where visual stimulation is kept to a minimum.

Reader Questions

1. **I am a teacher. It seems as if you want me to be on the lookout for all types of sensory disturbances in my children. What if I observe them, but the child appears to be handling his disturbance appropriately?** *I would say, then, that this child has developed his own particular coping mechanisms for his disorder. This is a good thing. What we want to be careful of, however, is that over- or underreactivity to sensory stimuli is not a setting-off event for someone else. Sometimes children with SPD can tolerate or even accommodate their own disturbances up to a certain point. I call that their threshold. Then, meltdown behavior will most likely occur. This means that if you continually expose the child to sensory stimuli without making accommodations with regard to the offending stimuli, you may actually be establishing grounds for a meltdown later with another teacher, in another classroom, or with Mom and Dad in the home setting.*

2. **Wow! Some of this is making sense! I do have some children who just can't sit still. But how do I get around the administration's requirement that we need to spend even more time on academics?** *You need to be as creative as you can*

to find ways to incorporate movement while the children sit in their seats. Perhaps you can create some desk exercises or stretching activities. You can also provide sensory input in additional ways, such as offering mints or juice breaks or incorporating music or chanting.

3. **How can I change a child's coordination inability? If he can't navigate steps, falls frequently, or has trouble in P.E., what should I do?** *You should refer him for an occupational therapy evaluation. Children who are this dysfunctional in school settings may not only need therapy, they may also require accommodations for their own safety.*

Chapter 5
Strategies to Address SPD

Children with sensory dysfunction need to be taught how sensory input can regulate their ability to be alert. This is a form of self-advocacy. For instance, if you are at work and you feel sleepy, you may get up to get a drink or take a short walk. If you are anxious, the same activities (get a drink or take a walk) may help you to calm down. An important part of incorporating sensory-integration strategies into the classroom is to provide awareness and self-advocacy skills to the student, so that he can learn to initiate his own set of activities to regulate his sensory system.

How Does Your Engine Run—The Alert Program for Self-Regulation, by Mary Sue Williams and Sherry Shellenberger (1994),[21] is an instructional program that helps children learn to become aware of their individual levels of alertness and initiate strategies to improve their attentiveness. Children learn to identify whether their energy "engines" are running low, high, or just right. To teach the children what engines in each stage feel like, various pictures accompany the levels. For instance, one picture depicts an anxious woman biting her fingernails. The child has to identify whether the woman's engine is on "high" or "low." Children are then taught specific things they can do to help them achieve optimal engine levels.

As adults, we have often learned through time and experience the things that we need to do to keep our sensory systems on track. For instance, when we need to be more alert, we may drink a caffeinated beverage. When we feel stressed, we often seek solitary, restful activities. Or, we may head to the gym for a strenuous workout. Assisting children in identifying and taking part in their own strategies is considered a positive support for children with SPD. When these activities are implemented in a systemized, planned way, we may refer to them as *sensory-diet activities:* They help to keep our sensory motors running appropriately.

Certain activities are thought to be calming activities for children with SPD. These include:

- Listening to soft music

- Listening to "white noise," such as the hum of a box fan

- Rocking slowly

- Engaging in deep breathing

- Chanting a mantra or a phrase

- Wrapping tightly in a blanket or sleeping bag

- Retreating into a tent, under a table covered by a long tablecloth, or behind a desk carrel (a desk with high sides meant to eliminate visual distractions; collapsible cardboard types are also available)

- Inhaling certain odors, such as lavender

- Sitting in a beanbag chair or between a pile of pillows

- Watching a lava lamp

- Engaging in self-hypnosis

- Using headphones or earphones in loud situations

- Using surgical gloves to avoid touching messy substances

- Wearing tight-fitting clothing, such as Under Armour (this type of clothing provides the student with proprioceptive input)

- Allowing the student to "retreat" into a hooded sweatshirt

As we mentioned earlier, there are many children who are underreactive to sensory stimuli. The above interventions may create a situation that further exacerbates a student's problems. Therefore, they may require activities that are more alerting or arousing. These children will derive benefit from the following:

- Opportunities to walk, run, and jump

- A supply of strongly flavored mints, candy, or gum

- Access to a personal water bottle

- Classroom materials that are brightly colored

- Writing implements that produce a variety of stimuli (glitter pens, smelly markers, gel pencils)

- Stress-reduction toys or "fidget toys" (**Figure 3**)

- Fresh air

- Brisk rubbing, brushing, tickling

- Strong smells

- Fewer "sitting" activities and more movement-based activities

Figure 3. Fidget toys should be given one at a time and followed up with a period of data collection to determine if use of the toy is beneficial.

So that we don't exacerbate problem behaviors, it is extremely important that we only include items in a child's sensory diet that have been deemed appropriate through data collection.

In Pennsylvania and many other states, it is now recognized under special-education law that a teacher or administrator cannot withhold a child's right to receive fresh air as a means to "punish" him for inappropriate behaviors. This particular special-education regulation becomes extremely important when we consider students who have sensory dysfunction. Eliminating a child's access to fresh air and opportunities to partake in gross-motor movements may, in fact, worsen a child's behavior if he is sensory impaired. If the child needs movement and fresh air to remain alert, calm, and focused, depriving him of recess as a form of punishment would not only be unfair, but it may also serve to exacerbate his problematic behaviors in the time period after recess. As many states are attempting to align their behavioral policies with IDEA, it is considered a basic student right not to be prevented access to food, water, or fresh air. For children with sensory dysfunction, withholding these essentials may inadvertently increase the number of episodes of problematic behavior. In other words, if a student needs to participate in recess to be able to maintain optimal alertness, then withholding recess only serves to ignite an already flammable fuel. This child will most likely increase his use of negative behaviors as he attempts to "rev" his system up to get the sensory input he craves.

Another problem that frequently surfaces with respect to special-education law concerns the use of food in the classroom as a reinforcer. Several states (Texas, California, and others) have established regulations that forbid the use of a *food with minimal nutritional value,* or FMNV, from being used in the classroom. The predominant reason why such laws have surfaced is a concern for childhood obesity. There are also concerns that many children have food-related allergies and that it may be life-threatening in some cases for these kids to be exposed to certain food substances. Many school districts have taken this law to the extreme, mandating that children with special needs cannot be provided with FMNV in the classroom as a means to reward positive behavior or to regulate sensory dysfunction. Such practices are not appropriate. If an IEP team designates an FMNV as being a positive reinforcer for a child or as a substance that would help keep the child in a state of appropriate sensory regulation, such a team decision could override school policy or even state law. IDEA is the federal law that governs the development of IEPs for children with special needs. Federal law always supersedes state law.

There may be other reasons why teachers and administrators are hesitant to use food or other types of sensory-diet items in the classroom. Many worry that these items might be appealing to typically developing kids and may cause dissention in the classroom because other children aren't getting them, too. As one teacher described, "I find it extremely hard to explain to the kids why Rick can have a mint to chew in class while he works and why the others can't because they don't have IEPs. It's just not fair to the other kids." One can look at this argument in several ways:

- The other kids do not have IEPs because they are not exceptional learners with SPD. Not providing a student with a sensory accommodation is about the same as ignoring his disability and expecting him to cope without assistance (ie, not allowing a child with vision problems to wear his glasses).

- As teachers, we must adjust our teaching methods to meet the needs of all students. If one of your children required seating up front because of poor vision, you would gladly do that. Having a ready-made answer for children who question your practices is often helpful. You must be confident in the delivery of your explanation; otherwise, the students may interpret that you disagree with the intervention, too. This will result in increased dissention in your classroom. A response such as, "Everyone gets what they need in my classroom. Someday, you will need something too, and I will provide it for you," would be appropriate, if delivered in a matter-of-fact, businesslike tone of voice.

- Some teachers feel that such questions are a violation of the disabled student's privacy and should not be addressed at all. If you feel this way, respond by saying, "This really isn't your concern. It's time to get back to work."

- Another option would be to choose a sensory-diet item that you would be comfortable providing for the entire class, such as a water bottle or a Wikki Stix (a piece of wax-coated string that is used as a fidget toy). The children who need a fidget item will hold onto the Wikki Stix and use it repeatedly. You may notice that their fidgety behaviors decrease and that they are more responsive and less distractible! Other children in your classroom will likely be less careful with it; often, you will find enough Wikki Stix on the floor to save and use for next year's distribution.

A word about water bottles: All children can better maintain optimal alertness when they are appropriately hydrated. In some parts of the country, having ready access to water is important, because many classrooms are still not air-conditioned. Having a water bottle at one's desk is probably one of the most effective sensory-related interventions that could benefit a child with sensory disturbance (either hyper- or hyposensitivity). A child who fidgets and is hypersensitive may require movement. He can get what he needs through gustatory and tactile input when he wraps his lips around the nozzle of the bottle and takes a drink. The water itself, as it passes through his lips and into his mouth and then flows down the back of his throat, also provides additional tactile and gustatory input. The water bottle, as well as the water, will serve to "rev" the child up.

If you are worried that a water bottle could spill and create more sensory problems with wet clothes or wet papers, only allow use of the sports-top models that have a pull-up plug. Make sure that the children have their name written on the bottle. Require that the bottle go home each night to be properly cleaned and refilled. (You will have to gain the cooperation of the parents to do this.) If you suspect that a student is using a dirty bottle that was not taken home at night, you can remove the bottle from his desk and allow him free access to the fountain for a preassigned number of visits or supply one of your own bottles for him to use. If you are worried about loss of grip or condensation, have the children cover the outside of the bottle with a sock. You can also prescribe the size of the bottle that you will accept in the classroom to avoid having water bottles that are huge and bulky.

A common intervention for reducing classroom noise is to insert tennis balls on the ends of the legs of chairs and/or desks. Drilling a small hole in the ball and then squeezing it to open the ball up makes it easier for the leg of a chair or desk to be inserted. Slicing the ball in the shape of an "X" with a box cutter works too, but they tend to fall off easier. Using the tennis balls eliminates the scraping and scratching noises when desks move or chairs are pushed in and out. Some teachers cover the balls with mismatched socks. When the socks become dirty, the students remove them, and they are then taken home to be washed.

There are many items that can be used at a child's desk to either provide movement for sensory seekers or serve as a calming device for sensory avoiders. One such device is a Thera-Band (a thin latex band) that can be tied to two desk legs (**Figure 4**). The child can push the band with his foot to feel resistance. This will give him some proprioceptive input.

Frequently, teachers report that there are certain students who just can't seem to sit in their seats. They may fall onto the floor several times a day, "perch" on their chairs, or sit on their feet. Their seating positions may be a source of irritation for their educators. Some of these children may have backsides that lack appropriate nerve endings. In other words, their rear ends may feel numb. This phenomenon may happen to many of us when we sit too long. If you can't feel the contact between your behind and a chair, you

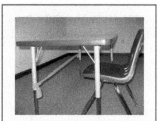

Figure 4. A Thera-Band can be tied between two desk legs to provide proprioceptive input for a student with SPD.

Figure 5. An inflatable disk such as this one can provide sensory input for a child with SPD as he sits in his chair.

will obviously have trouble sitting on it. One recommendation could be having the child sit on an inflatable disk that has raised bumps (**Figure 5**). This may curb his urge to wiggle. Or, he or she could use a therapy ball instead of a desk chair to help regulate attention and the proprioceptive sense. Some teachers have also tried a weighted vest. This is simply a vest that contains pockets. Small pouches of weighted material such as rice or beans are then inserted into the pockets. The theory behind the use of these is to provide increased tactile pressure for the students. You can also purchase weighted lap pads that use the same concept: Pouches of weighted material are sewn into a small pad that the student lays across his lap.

If a child has difficulty understanding where his personal space is in relation to others, defining his seating area with masking tape, a carpet square, or a towel or designating it in some other visual way may be helpful. If desks are pushed up against each other to form a table arrangement, using brightly colored electrical tape to outline his desk may help him "see" his boundaries.

As was mentioned earlier, giving a student a fidget toy can be useful to provide movement to sensory seekers, but these items can also serve as calming tools. Fidget toys can be just about anything that a child can hold or manipulate in his hand: marbles, small flat stones, rubber bracelets, Isoflex balls, Wikki Stix, Slinkies, Koosh balls, squeeze toys, pipe cleaners, jacks, or a bendable drinking straw. Some children have adopted their own fidget toys.

Martin, a 10-year-old boy with autism, frequently carries around the spring from a ballpoint pen. His mom and dad shared with

the school that if Martin is allowed to have
this spring in the school setting, they believe it
will keep him from going into sensory overload.
Martin has a history of meltdown behavior when
he gets too overwhelmed by sensory stimuli. One
of Martin's teachers is not in favor of him having
the spring in class. She believes it is a distraction.
All of Martin's other teachers allow him to
have it. Data collection revealed that Martin's
behavior is better in the classrooms in which
he is allowed to have the spring, versus the one
classroom in which he is not. This data could be
useful for getting the reluctant teacher to give in;
however, it is not foolproof. His behavior could
be worse in this class because it is also a difficult
subject for him. Or, it could also be that Martin
does not adapt well to this educator's particular
teaching style. However, it would be useful to try
the strategy and record data in her class to see if
Martin's problem behaviors diminished!

Even allowing a student to run an errand for you can be helpful. Having him carry a box that is somewhat heavy to another part of the building can provide some proprioceptive input. Some teachers collaborate with office staff to have the student perform various errands during the school day to achieve this extra movement. The student may be asked to carry sealed envelopes (empty, of course!) to the office to get a break from sitting too long.

As mentioned previously, when sensory-diet items are added to a child's day with the hope of eliminating sensory-related behaviors, confirm each choice by means of data collection to ensure that it is indeed making a difference. Implement one intervention at a time, and go about this in a scientific manner, studying the effects (positive or negative) before implementing another. If sensory interventions are applied haphazardly, with reckless disregard as to whether they work or not, it will be hard for teachers to support using them. Educators cannot become "vested" in the use of these items if they are unsure about their effects on classroom behavior. Only data collection will confirm their usefulness; and if it does not, these items may serve as nothing more than distractions for the student with SPD, as well as for the other kids. As mentioned earlier, the implementation of some sensory-diet items may actually worsen a child's behavior, if not in the immediate venue, then later in the day, during another subject or in another classroom. Collecting data is the only way to determine the effectiveness of sensory-diet items.

Making Your Own Fidget Toys

What you will need:

Some round latex balloons

A funnel

A bag of rice, small pasta, or tiny uncooked beans

A large, empty shoe box or gift box

Directions:

Pour the rice, pasta, or beans into the shoe box. Place the mouth of the balloon over the bottom of the funnel. Scoop some rice, pasta, or beans into the funnel with your hands. (This will serve as a sensory activity for the student! Be aware that some children with SPD will enjoy this, while others will not.) The balloon will begin to fill up. You may need to shake it slightly to keep the opening from getting clogged. Tie off the balloon. Using different types of materials inside the balloon also provides different tactile input for sensory seekers! Consider trying sugar, sand, flour, birdseed, cat litter, beads, or anything else that will fit through the neck of the balloon (**Figure 6**).

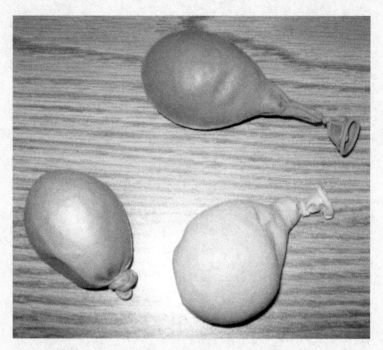

Figure 6. Fidget toys made out of balloons provide a discreet form of sensory input in the classroom. Some children with SPD will enjoy helping to make them!

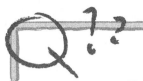

Reader Questions

1. **I think making my children stay in from recess when they have not listened is good classroom management. It works every time! No one likes to miss recess. I am still not convinced I should stop this practice.** *If having your children stay in for recess does not serve as a setting-off event for more problematic behavior in the time period afterward, then, obviously, this particular technique works for you. What you need to make sure of, however, is that you read the IEPs or 504 plans of the children you have in your classroom to make sure that you are in compliance with those documents. Your own particular classroom-management activities should not override an IEP or 504 team's decision.*

2. **I frequently have to address the individual needs of students who have disabilities in my classroom, and sometimes it does cause some protest from the other kids. They think the child is getting preferential treatment. Is there anything else you can suggest other than the items you mention in the book?** *Be sure to point out when you are providing an accommodation to the other students. They will take notice! As an example, if you typically do not allow children to get drinks in the middle of class,*

the next time a student asks, you could preface your response by saying, "Well, you know the rule. I don't allow drinks. However, you do look a little dehydrated. Go ahead and get a drink." When the kids begin to realize that you care about all of their needs, your point will be made.

3. **I have tried some of these sensory-diet items because the mother of one of my students insists that they help her son. Frankly, I have not seen a change in his behavior. How can I convey that to her without causing a rift in our relationship? She is rather demanding. So far, I have always attempted to accommodate her wishes for the sake of her child.** *Good for you! When teachers and parents can work together to brainstorm solutions to problems, it is a win-win situation for both the student and his educators. Some parents take teacher comments personally. If you tell Mom that the sensory diet just didn't work, she may be doubtful that you even tried it. However, if you can show her at least 2 weeks' worth of data to support your comments, you take the "personal" out of it. You might try saying something like this: "I was eager to try the sensory-diet items you suggested. I wanted to see if they would help to reduce the number of meltdowns your son is having in the classroom. So, we implemented the things*

you suggested and recorded data for 2 weeks by using a frequency count. As you can see by my chart here, the number of meltdowns did not change. In fact, they worsened. Do you have any ideas of what we can try next?" If you did not have the data to support what you were saying to mom, she might misinterpret your comments to mean that you just weren't interested in implementing the diet.

4. **So how long should I try these sensory-diet items?** *I would say that you should try each item in isolation for at least 2 weeks. You want to be certain which ones are effective and which ones aren't.*

Chapter 6

Creating a Sensory Room within Your School or Classroom

Because it is often difficult to create a sensory-friendly classroom that is appropriate for the needs of each student, it may be helpful to create a sensory room or an area apart from your classroom in the school building. Such a room could serve as a place that could benefit many children with SPD.

The most important thing to consider when creating a sensory room is to make sure that this room does not get used as a "time-out" room. Staff members should take all precautions that this area is not associated with problematic behavior. Indeed, it is most helpful to use the area proactively. For instance, if you suspect that a student is becoming agitated, it may be a good idea to visit the sensory room for some downtime. Waiting until the meltdown occurs to remove him from the classroom may be conceived as a punishment. He may then refuse to go. Another issue of concern is that some students do not like to leave work unfinished. They are fearful that they will miss something if they leave the room. Making a visit to the sensory room a regular part of his day, *which he can see on a visual schedule that is reviewed with him at the start of each day,* may be helpful. If you or the student is worried about missing instructional time, utilize the room after a shortened recess or lunch period.

If an established time of day is not designated for the sensory room, another problem might arise. Many teachers provide their students with "break cards." The students can present their cards when they need a "break" and are requesting an opportunity to leave the classroom and visit the sensory area. Kids being kids, they may learn to use their "break cards" whenever they don't want to complete a nonpreferred activity. Thus, they may try to manipulate their teachers to avoid work. If they are allowed to leave, requesting a "break" during such activities will become habitual. Their teachers will inadvertently be reinforcing escape from such tasks if they allow them to leave.

If you have discovered through data collection that your student becomes tired and lethargic in the later part of the day, scheduling a visit to the sensory room to obtain sensory input prior to beginning a task that will require alertness could make him more productive. Confirm this through data collection by counting the number of prompts your student needs to maintain attention to task on days when he does attend the room versus days that he does not. Or, compare grades on work completed after he visits the sensory room with work completed on days when he did not visit the room. Interval-sampling data collection to note off-task behavior or self-stimulatory behavior during the hour that immediately follows a visit to the sensory room would also be useful in determining if he derived benefit from using the room.

A visit to the sensory room could also be warranted before times of the day that involve difficult subjects for the student. Naturally, as educators, you want the child to be operating at optimal attention levels during such times.

If your data collection shows that your student has frequent behavioral problems when he has been overly stimulated (such as after recess or lunch), then schedule his sensory-room participation after those modules. Utilize the previously mentioned methods of data collection to determine if this has been helpful.

If you are using a visual transition schedule, the student will know when it is time to visit the sensory area and not abuse the privilege. By "scheduling" a visit to the room, rather than allowing him to request attendance to this area at random, you will be avoiding accidentally reinforcing escape. In this way, other children can use the room during their scheduled times, as well. Speech therapists and occupational therapists can use their expertise to service children individually or within groups as they use the sensory area.

> *Mason had SPD. His school used a sensory room to address the needs of children like him. Mason frequently requested to visit the room when academic activities became difficult. He was already on "overload" when he asked to use the room. Through data collection, Mason's IEP team found that Mason's visits to the room were becoming more frequent, and he often left the room during written-expression assignments and during the math module. Since Mason's retreat served as an escape from this type of work, he learned to request to use the sensory room more frequently. Mason's team decided to utilize a more scheduled approach to his use of the room. Mason began to visit the room* before *math and written expression so that he would be functioning with an optimal level of calmness when he initiated these types of tasks. In addition, Mason's skill set was also examined. After a psychological assessment, it was discovered that Mason's math ability was two grade levels below that of his peers. Accommodations and adaptations were going to be necessary for him to be successful in this subject. Further, since Mason suffered from fine-motor deficits, writing*

assignments were often a source of frustration. His team decided that Mason would be provided with the opportunity to compose his written-expression assignments on a computer. Graphic organizers were used, along with preteaching exercises, to improve his organizational skills when completing writing assignments. All of these interventions proved useful in helping Mason to be on-task and give his best effort.

Occasionally, a team will become concerned that a student is not able to finish all of his work if he goes to the sensory room. Indeed, this may cause added tension for kids that have an awareness and concern for what their peers can do versus what they can do. As mentioned previously, these same kids may worry about their grades and falling behind. At this point, the team needs to compare the preintervention data with the postintervention data. If the child is definitely able to concentrate and perform better with the intervention in place, then it might be necessary to reduce the amount of work that he is required to do on returning to the classroom, as opposed to that of his peers. For example, his worksheet could be shortened, or he could be asked to do every other problem. His worksheet should not be compared with those of other students, as this will draw attention to the differences in his sheet.

Some professionals suggest that missed work should be sent home or completed at another time, such as at recess. This is strongly *not* recommended. Since many children with SPD are also learning disabled, homework takes much longer. It is often viewed as a punishment. And, as we have seen previously, holding him back from recess may exacerbate sensory-related behaviors. Modifying his work is a better way to go. If he is showing mastery of key concepts because he has taken the sensory break, then you have accomplished what you set out to do. If the intervention has been shown to work by means of data collection, then, by all means, attempt to keep it in place. Reviewing a visual schedule at the start of the child's day and showing the child when he may visit the sensory room would be a matter-of-fact approach to having him leave the classroom. This may serve to reduce refusals to leave. Providing him with a positive reinforcer as he completes each module of his schedule leading up to the sensory-room visit will also reduce arguments about going.

Figure 7. Jumping on a small trampoline is a good way to wake up and become more alert!

When visiting the sensory room, the student should be guided to activities in the room that would best suit his individual sensory needs. For instance, if he is experiencing a heightened state of alertness after a noisy gym class, he could go into a tent and listen to quiet music with headphones. If he appears to be sleepy and needs to become more alert, encouraging him to jump on a trampoline may be more effective **(Figure 7)**. A good way to discern if a child is ready to return to his classroom would be to have him complete a puzzle or similar activity. If he is able to do so relatively easily and without a lot of prompts or frustration, this is a good indicator that he is ready to return.

Many occupational therapists are integrating a form of skin-brushing into their sensory-integration programs. This intervention should always be performed with the guidance and instruction of an occupational therapist.

The brushing technique (often referred to as the Wilbarger Brushing Technique, developed in 1991 by Patricia Wilbarger, an internationally recognized occupational therapist specializing in sensory integration) is performed by using a surgical brush. Surgical brushes have soft plastic bristles and are often used by surgeons for "scrubbing up" prior to performing surgery. These are often the brushes used when attempting to normalize tactile sensitivity because they will not scratch the skin. The occupational therapist will brush the child's back, legs, arms, and soles of the feet by using a firm, horizontal motion. The face, neck, stomach, and chest should not be brushed. Contrary to popular opinion, it is not the brushing that helps calm the child's tactile defensiveness. It is the administration of pressure on the brush. If done correctly, this serves as a form of deep massage, and this is believed to be what calms the child. It has been said that the results of the brushing calm the child for up to 90 minutes and that when applying the technique at home, the family needs to perform the brushing six to eight times a day. Each application of brushing should be followed by joint compression—squeezing the joints of the shoulder, elbows, wrists, hips, knees, and feet to provide proprioceptive input. The entire routine should only take about 3 minutes.

Again, as with all sensory-integration techniques, there is much anecdotal and observational evidence that this technique works, but little is backed with solid research data. Many parents and teachers report that children who are brushed are often calmer and more attentive and have fewer meltdowns. Many times, brushing is done prior to engaging in any other sensory-related activities in the sensory-integration room.

When setting up your sensory room, try to include items that pertain to the individual sensory needs of your students. Items to include in your sensory room may include things that provide relaxation and reduce sensory overload, as well as those that may provide sensory feedback to recharge a child's "engine."

Sensory items to relax and reduce sensory input:
- Pop-up tent or table with a long tablecloth
- Beanbag chair (**Figure 8**)
- Suspended platform swing (**Figure 9**)

- Rocking chair
- Blanket to wrap a child in
- Sheepskin or "fur" rugs
- Floor mats
- Tape recorder with headphones
- Tapes of soft music and/or nature sounds
- Lava lamp
- Tabletop fountains
- Fish tank
- Stress-reducing squeeze toys
- Weighted vest, lap pad, or neck roll
- Yoga videotape/VCR/TV

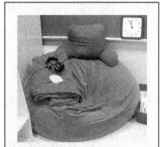

Figure 8. A beanbag chair is an ideal spot to have some sensory downtime and to read a book or maybe listen to some quiet music.

Sensory items to provide additional sensory input:
- Trampoline for jumping
- Therapy ball for bouncing
- Room-darkening blinds
- Disco ball
- Black lights—try to include a lot of white items in the room for contrast!
- Plasma balls
- Bubble machines
- Selection of gum/mints/tart candy/drinks/water
- Teeter-totter or scooter

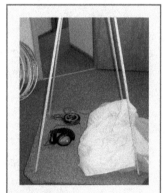

Figure 9. A platform swing offers some quiet relaxation.

- Fabric squares doused with scents (cinnamon, peppermint, lemon)— store each in a Tupperware container!

- Water, sand, or rice table—also experiment with Insta-Snow (a substance that resembles snow when mixed with water) (**Figure 10**)

Figure 10. A low table can be created to allow a child access to sand, water, rice, or even Insta-Snow for some additional sensory input.

- Vibrating toys/chairs

- Squishy toys

- Ball pit (**Figure 11**)

- Mobiles to hang on the ceiling

- Spinning toys

- Sit 'n Spin

- Small indoor sandbox (of box of dry beans or rice) (**Figure 12**)

Figure 11. A small ball pit can be used to provide sensory input during the school day.

For many reasons, it may not be beneficial or even feasible to have a child removed from the classroom to report to a sensory room. There are many ways that a sensory area can be established within a classroom, as well.

In many elementary-school classrooms, there are movable pieces of furniture that can serve as separators from regular seating areas. Perhaps a bookshelf can be arranged as such a separator. A sensory

Figure 12. You can make a small, indoor sandbox by placing sand (or dry beans or rice) in a large Tupperware container!

area can consist of a card table with a tablecloth draped over it, a carpet, a beanbag chair, some headphones, and a tape recorder for playing soft music. Various stress-reducing toys and textures could also be provided for the child (**Figure 13**). One teacher the author works with uses a collapsible children's tent for the students to retreat to (**Figure 14**). This keeps all the materials in a confined area. Some classrooms are large enough to accommodate a small trampoline or therapy ball to bounce on. These items could be used to provide sensory input when "revving up" is needed. A small timer can remind the student that it's time to get back to work. If he complies when the timer goes off, he could earn a reinforcer so that he learns not to abuse the sensory area or use it as a form of escape. (It will be hard to return to work when the sensory area is very relaxing!)

Teachers do not have to spend a lot of money to establish a sensory area in their classroom. Many educators report that they are able to find sensory items at garage sales or even around their own homes. Creativity can go far when the financial resources are just not available.

Figure 13. Different textures can be made available to the child in the sensory area, such as this "fuzzy cat"—a painted cat on the wall with white fur glued to its belly, a real rhinestone collar, and vinyl paws.

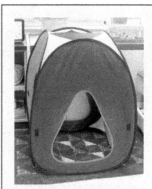

Figure 14. A collapsible tent like this one serves as the perfect classroom retreat.

Reader Questions

1. **I have a student who gets very stressed about getting behind in his work and/or looking different from his peers. He could really benefit from using a de-stress room, but I know he would refuse to go. He does not want to look different from his peers!** *Visual schedules can work really nicely in this sort of situation. A visual schedule is just that—a schedule of the student's day, displayed pictorially. The sensory room is built into the schedule. It is not used as a punishment or during times when the student is having a meltdown. It's a matter-of-fact way to "show" the child that this is how things are going to go for the day. He is less likely to argue when it becomes a regular part of his day.*

2. **My school doesn't have an empty space that they can dedicate to becoming a sensory room, and neither does my classroom. Any ideas for us?** *Yes! The author has visited schools that have dedicated an area by using a partition behind a stage curtain. Others have utilized a partition to set off an area in a book-storage room. One school used the guidance office for a sensory room, as the guidance counselor is only in the building one day per week. I have even*

seen dedicated sensory areas in the speech or occupational therapy room, behind a computer lab, or in a learning-support classroom.

3. **I'm worried that kids will abuse the sensory area if I set it up in my classroom. They may object to returning to their seats!** *You will have to set up rules for the use of the sensory area, just like everything else you do in your classroom. With observation, you will also begin to tell which children need longer periods there and which kids don't.*

Chapter 7
Self-Stimulatory and Self-Abusive Behavior—The Connection to SPD

Self-Stimulatory Behavior

Many children utilize self-stimulatory behavior to keep themselves regulated. Self-stimulatory behavior may also be referred to as stereotypical behavior. To be stereotypical, it must be repetitive in nature. Self-stimulatory behavior may consist of one or more of the following:

- Rocking
- Smacking lips
- Making mouth noises
- Picking nose/lips/skin
- Flicking things in front of the eyes
- Hand flapping/slapping
- Humming
- Repeating phrases to oneself
- Spinning
- Sniffing objects or people
- Putting objects in the mouth or sucking on objects
- Excessive blinking

We often acquaint self-stimulatory behavior with children who have disabilities. However, all individuals engage in such behavior at one time or another. Self-stimulatory behavior serves a purpose for the student. If the student has been successful using self-stimulatory behavior to fulfill that purpose, the student is more likely to engage in the self-stimulatory behavior again.

Individuals without disabilities exhibit self-stimulatory behavior for various reasons. Consider people who are attending a seminar. The longer the attendees must sit, the more likely they will engage in self-stimulatory behavior. They utilize these behaviors, unintentionally, to maintain a certain level of alertness. Otherwise, they might drift off to sleep! Such behavior may take the form of hair-twirling, feet-tapping, leg-wiggling, or flicking pens or pencils. Because these are socially appropriate behaviors, for the most part, they go unnoticed. Occasionally, self-stimulatory behavior that is socially appropriate to some may be bothersome to others. Perhaps the individuals who are bothered by it may have their own sensory disturbances! Most of us, at one time or another, have experienced a person whose self-stimulatory behavior is annoying. An individual who cracks his chewing gum is an example. A chewing-gum popper is most likely someone who is using gustatory, tactile, and auditory input to keep himself attentive. A person seated next to him on one side may not even notice the sound. Another may notice it but be able to tune it out. For some, though, the cracking sound will be an annoyance that interferes with attention and learning. For these same individuals, their own auditory sensitivity may cause them difficulty as they attempt to inhibit the sounds of another's self-stimulatory behavior!

Some children with SPD also engage in self-stimulatory behaviors to "keep their engines running." Their behaviors may look socially appropriate, as in the previous examples, or they may take on one or more of the behaviors in the list provided at the beginning of this chapter. These children need movement to be able to pay attention.

This would be a good opportunity to discuss on-task behavior. As we have mentioned earlier, the longer an individual has to sit, the more he will find it difficult to attend, unless he is engaged in some activity that involves more than just listening. Second graders, for instance, are most likely able to sit somewhere between 10 and 15 minutes before they become distracted and begin to squirm. For children with disabilities, this time frame is probably going to be less. The author urges teachers to consider the rule of having the child remain seated for 1 minute per each of the child's years of age. (Example: A 7-year-old can sit for 7 minutes.) Although this is often a lofty goal to achieve in today's classroom, if educators have an awareness of the appropriate length of seated time, they will be more proactive about scheduling movement breaks. Breaking up extended seated periods with movement-based activities will help to keep the child functioning at optimal attention levels. This will in turn improve his academic functioning.

Some children and adults with sensory disturbance may engage in self-stimulatory behaviors to escape from sensory input. For children with auditory sensitivity, an increase in such behaviors results from exposure to loud noises or chaotic environments. Physical-education classes are an example: The echoing of shouts and whistles within the confines of a gymnasium may be too much for the child. Music modules, including band and chorus, may be problematic. Pep rallies, sporting events, programs and assemblies, or even loud classroom activities may send the child into overload. Thus, the student may engage in self-stimulatory behaviors to escape the sensory commotion. However, it's not just an overload of the auditory sense that some children may need to escape from. A keen sense of smell may also be problematic. Many of us have had the unpleasant experience of sitting next to someone whose perfume was intense, or maybe their body odor was offensive. It is difficult to ignore unpleasant smells, and sometimes we simply must move our seats. Other times, we might try to endure it by covering our noses with our hands so that we can only smell our own skin. So it is for children with SPD. Without proper coping abilities, they attempt to shut out the offensive stimuli (auditory, olfactory, gustatory, visual, tactile) with self-stimulatory behavior.

As mentioned previously, children will often engage in self-stimulatory behavior when they are anxious. A child can become anxious when his environment becomes too much of a sensory challenge for him, but it is also more likely to happen when the sensory challenge is unpredictable. If one is "on-edge" because of the anticipation of an unpleasant sensory experience, one will have a heightened anxiety level, especially if there is a memory of a preexisting event. Problematic behavior may result from the anxiety associated with the event itself, or because of the *expectation* of such an event.

> *Mark was frightened of loud noises. His IEP stated that fire drills would most likely result in meltdown behaviors for Mark. The IEP called for Mark to be removed from his classroom prior to a fire drill, and it had been arranged for Mark to eat his meals outside the cafeteria, in a quiet room. For this reason, alternative arrangements would also be made for school assemblies or class parties. Mark had a substitute teacher one day when the fire drill went off. Mark threw himself on the floor, writhing in pain. He held his ears and screamed, and began biting his arm. It took three staff members to carry him out. The next day, while riding to school on the bus, Mark began to get agitated. When the bus door opened to allow the children to proceed into the school, Mark ran down the bus steps and into the nearby woods. It took staff members an hour to retrieve*

him, and eventually, they had to send him home because he was too upset to attend his classes. Mark's behavior was a learned response to the sensory assault he had experienced the day before. For weeks afterwards, Mark engaged in an increased number of self-stimulatory behaviors and appeared to be "jumpy" in his classroom.

Many parents report that during times of stress, their children exhibit more self-stimulatory behaviors than at other times. Self-stimulatory behaviors may be more prevalent when a child is attempting to complete something that is difficult for him, and this may or may not have anything to do with sensory input. There are also individuals who engage in self-stimulatory behavior as a way to cope with increased demands. Transitions, changes in environment or materials, work that is too difficult, testing situations, and social demands may also serve to increase a student's use of self-stimulatory behavior.

Another reason for self-stimulatory behavior may come from a lack of appropriate skills to complete a given task or participate in a given activity. For instance, during unstructured time, a student may not possess the necessary skills to socialize with peers. He may lack executive-function skills that would enable him to be able to organize what he has to do next. Thus, observers may see more self-stimulatory behavior during "downtime," such as while the student is waiting in line, when he is left to work independently, when there is freedom to socialize in the classroom, or when he is waiting for instruction to begin. These students frequently lack the ability to glean what is expected of them during such times. Since they do not have the skill set to initiate a more appropriate behavior, they resort to "stimming."

Meagan had mild retardation and frequently engaged in spitting. When her behavioral support team conducted some analysis of the behavior, they found that Meagan would spit when she was attempting difficult academic tasks and also when left alone to converse with her peers.

Justin's middle-school art teacher complained that Justin frequently engaged in spinning while waiting for class to begin. The other students would point and laugh at Justin, and she felt the spinning was causing some disruption to her classroom. The behavioral specialist believed that Justin lacked the ability to initiate his work without adult intervention. She also observed that he lacked the appropriate skills to engage in social interactions with his peers prior to the start of his classes or while walking to and from his classes in the hallways. The transition to the art room might also be causing some stress for Justin. Justin's new behavioral plan included many types of supports: A speech therapist worked with him to learn to initiate and sustain conversations, a visual schedule was introduced to reduce transition anxiety, and a visual task list was provided for Justin to complete at the start of each period so that he knew what he was supposed to do before instruction began.

Teachers frequently report through data collection that children have more difficulty avoiding self-stimulatory behavior when they are not engaged (ie, waiting for the teacher to finish "housekeeping" duties, such as performing attendance checks or cafeteria counts or filling out hall passes). When a student has social as well as sensory difficulties, there may be more self-stimulatory behavior at lunch or recess. Such children can often be observed walking the perimeter instead of engaging with peers. During these times, it might be helpful to try other types of interventions—perhaps teaching the child a new skill or engaging him in another way.[22] Again, this is all the more reason why data collection is important, so that we can design effective interventions for such children.

Probably the most important piece of advice about addressing self-stimulatory behaviors is to ascertain if they are interfering with the child's learning or the learning of others. If they are, then considering the implementation of some interventions would be appropriate. If you want to address the behaviors merely because they "look different," you may be heading down a slippery slope.

> *Tessa had Down syndrome. She frequently slapped her thighs. Her teacher felt that the behavior was odd and wanted it to stop. It didn't seem to be disturbing the other students, but Tessa's teacher believed that it should be addressed. Each time Tessa slapped her thighs, her teacher would say in a sharp tone of voice, "NO!" and hold her hands down. Tessa began to get aggressive with her teacher—something she had never done previously. Whenever she approached Tessa's desk, Tessa spat at her or reached out to hit her. Clearly, stopping Tessa's slapping had resulted in a heightened form of stress for her.*

Many educators have noticed that when they have attempted to stop a self-stimulatory behavior, the child may then engage in another behavior that is worse. This is because the child's self-stimulatory behavior was serving a purpose for him or her. Preventing the behavior resulted in the child having to engage in a replacement behavior that was even more socially inappropriate than the first. Therefore, it is important for the educator to create a *substitute* behavior that may be more socially appropriate but also serve the same function for the student.

If the child is doing something with his hands, then providing him with a stress-reduction toy, similar to the ones in chapter 6, could be useful. In this way, his hands can be used to provide the same sort of input, but in a more socially appropriate way.

> *Kurt frequently engaged in finger-snapping. His occupational therapist provided him with a rubber bracelet to wear on his wrist. He could snap this bracelet, and it would not make the distracting noise associated with finger snapping.*

If the child engages in smelling activities, providing a controlled smelling activity may give him the olfactory input he craves. For instance, he may respond well to using scented pens and paper. He may also benefit from applying a scented lotion. For some children, engaging in an activity that provides olfactory stimulation may actually increase his or her attentiveness. However, one must be careful about incorporating olfactory-based activities. It is often difficult to discern if the student is craving smell, disturbed by a smell, or smelling something as a means of reassuring himself that the item or the expectations associated with that item have not changed. Providing additional olfactory experiences for such a child may create additional problems.

> *Maggie had an overreactive sense of smell. Her teacher frequently wore perfume and Bath & Body Works hand lotions. Often, Maggie became irritated and sometimes nauseated in class. To her, the light aroma was an explosion to her olfactory sense. Maggie smelled her papers and materials in this class more often than she did in other classrooms. She also exhibited other types of self-stimulatory behavior and at higher frequencies during periods when she worked with this teacher.*

Or consider the following:

> Evan was a junior-high student who had
> profound retardation and was nonverbal. His
> aggressive behaviors were on the rise. His IEP
> team could not discover the reason, and data
> collection had not proven useful, as no clear
> hypothesis could be confirmed. The team was
> about to meet to brainstorm some additional
> ideas when his mother noticed a Glade Plug-In
> air freshener in the electric socket of the wall near
> Evan's seat. She asked the teacher about this.
> The teacher said that frequently, her students
> avoided using deodorants (perhaps also for
> sensory reasons!), and she used the air freshener
> to provide relief. Evan's mom informed the team
> that smells were difficult for Evan at times. She
> suggested that they remove the air freshener
> and record some data to see if the number of
> his aggressive behaviors diminished. The team
> decided to follow her advice. And guess what—
> Mom was right!

Some of us can remember a time during our school years when our teachers passed out a handout that was duplicated through the use of a spirit duplicator, commonly referred to as a ditto machine. It was hard to resist the temptation to put the ditto to our noses and sniff! Smelling the odor of the spirits was often a "pick-me-up," and sniffing the paper probably served as an arousal-type behavior. Thus, some children can be provided with "pick-me-up" types of smells (citrus, mint, cinnamon) and may appear more attentive afterwards.

> Corbin had autism. He loved the smell of Herbal
> Essence shampoo. Corbin also appeared to be
> hyposensitive to many sensory stimuli. Sometimes,

when he appeared sleepy, his teacher would allow him to unscrew the top of an Herbal Essence shampoo bottle and take a whiff. Immediately, Corbin became more alert. She also provided Corbin with baggies of lemon and orange peel to sniff. She believed that implementing strategies to encourage olfactory stimulation improved his attention.

Sometimes, in lieu of data collection or while data collection is ongoing, it is helpful in a pinch to encourage a replacement behavior when the self-stimulatory behavior involves a distracting gross-motor movement (kicking the foot, tapping the hands, slapping the thighs). As mentioned earlier, if a child is kicking his table rungs or chair rungs, attaching a vinyl Thera-Band tightly to two rungs may create some proprioceptive input as he pushes with his feet and feels the resistance. This child, too, could probably benefit from some additional seated sensory activities. Frequently, a child may engage in rocking or rhythmical motions to provide input to his proprioceptive system. The same type of input could be created by having the student sit on a therapy ball or a seat cushion. Allowing the child specific times to engage in rocking (such as using a rocking chair in the sensory room) will also help him learn that it's okay to rock at certain times of the day but not at others. Providing him with additional movement-based activities may also reduce the child's need to rock.

As we have seen previously, sometimes a self-stimulatory behavior does bother others and interferes with the instructor's ability to create a classroom conducive to learning. At such times, self-stimulatory behavior needs to be addressed. For instance, a complaint commonly occurs when a child hums constantly. This child may be trying to give some gustatory input to his sensory system. Allowing the child opportunities to provide vibration to his mouth area may be helpful. Perhaps he could use a kazoo, an electric toothbrush, or personal massager. (Of course, these strategies would not be used in the classroom, but perhaps there could be some time devoted to providing this gustatory input in other parts of the day.) If he is attempting to shut out noises with the humming, permitting him to wear earplugs to decrease noise in the environment may be helpful. Data collection will confirm which intervention will work.

If a student is smacking his lips or making any other type of mouth sounds, we might hypothesize that he is also seeking gustatory input. Such a child may benefit from some extra gustatory stimulation. Examples would be flavored lip balm or lip gloss; Altoid mints (because of their very strong taste); cinnamon, lemon, or "popping" candy; a water bottle; chewing gum; an opportunity to brush his teeth with mint toothpaste; or the use of strong mouthwash or carbonated or "tart" beverages.

When a child chews on clothing, nails, pens, or pencils, giving him chewy and crunchy snacks, such as pretzels, gummy bears, or chewing gum, may be helpful. This would be one way to give the child the oral input he needs.

If a child is pulling his hair out or plucking the fibers of his clothes, having him wear incompatible clothing for plucking behavior (such as gloves) may be helpful. It should be noted that pulling one's hair out repeatedly could be a symptom of trichotillomania, which is actually a form of self-abusive behavior. Oftentimes, children with this disorder may have a coexisting condition, such as obsessive-compulsive disorder, generalized anxiety disorder, or mood disorder. Medical intervention will be necessary in the form of medication management, as well as therapy. If the child tends to pull his hair out during sedentary activities, incorporating frequent sensory breaks, as well as sensory-diet items at his seat, may help to reduce this behavior.

Masturbation

Another socially inappropriate behavior in the classroom is masturbation. This is one of the most difficult behaviors to address because of the high level of sensory input that is achieved from participation in this activity. Students who engage in this behavior often have no awareness that what they are doing is inappropriate. Besides giving the child additional sensory input to his tactile and proprioceptive systems, teaching the child the difference between public behavior and private behavior is important. The child has to learn that touching one's genitals is a *private behavior,* and private behaviors can only be initiated in *private places* (ie, the child's bedroom or bathroom at home). Sometimes a *social scenario* can be reviewed with the child, such as the one provided at the end of this chapter. These little scenarios are designed to teach a replacement behavior. By reviewing the scenario with the child, you may help him to learn a more socially appropriate way to meet his sensory needs. In the classroom, it may be helpful to give the child more opportunities for movement, especially with aerobic exercise. Having him sit with a weighted lap pad or wear a weighted vest may also help to eliminate this behavior. Increasing the amount of tactile input through the use of fidget toys, Koosh balls, or Velcro strips attached to his desk may also be useful.

Self-Abusive Behavior

Self-abusive or self-injurious behavior is behavior that a student engages in that causes harm to himself. When a child's self-stimulatory behavior crosses over into self-abusive behavior (as in the hair-pulling instance above), a more conscientious effort has to be made on the part of staff members to discover by means of data collection what may be driving the behavior. Functional behavioral assessments then become critical components in the child's educational plan. Consider the following example:

Alex has mental retardation. Frequently, when he is placed in a highly stimulating environment (such as riding the bus to school or going on a field trip), he will engage in self-abusive behavior. He will slap himself in the head or bite his hands and arms. His parents have attempted to explain to his teachers that when his environment is too stimulating (noisy, confusing, or lacking structure), they have observed that he will initiate these behaviors. His parents provided Alex with a stress-reduction toy to hold on the bus. However, his teacher routinely has Alex deposit the toy in a box as he enters the classroom—she believes that the toy makes him look different from his peers and serves as a distraction to him. This has resulted in increased instances of biting for Alex, as well as tissue damage.

In this example, Alex's teacher does not understand that for some children, stress-reduction toys are necessary accommodations, and that self-abusive behavior is not something to ignore. Reducing the frequency of self-abusive behaviors always must take precedence over academic performance.

Frequently, students who engage in such behaviors have mental retardation and may be limited in terms of communicating their wants and needs. When self-abusive behavior results in tissue damage, it is vital that the behavior be studied by means of a functional behavioral analysis so that appropriate strategies can be recommended. Such behaviors can cause serious injury and/or permanent damage, and they deserve the attention of a behavioral expert with experience in dealing with this type of behavior.

As mentioned previously, some children become so frustrated with an inability to communicate their needs and wants that they resort to self-abusive behaviors. In these instances, it is vital that students be provided with a functional form of communication or a system that works for them. Picture-communication boards, computers, electronic communication devices, and sign language are all examples of such systems.

> *Meghan has Down syndrome. She developed a habit of hitting and biting herself, especially when frustrated. The team Meghan worked with at school last year began to teach her sign language. As a result, the number of Meghan's self-abusive and self-stimulatory behaviors decreased. This year, however, Meghan is attending a new school. Her new teachers do not know sign language. Meghan is again resorting to an increase in the use of self-abusive behaviors. Clearly, she could benefit from her teachers being trained in sign language so they can communicate with her more effectively.*

Sometimes, the self-abusive behavior takes the form of skin-picking. Some therapists speculate that the child may be engaging in the behavior to calm himself. Adding calming activities to this student's sensory diet may be helpful. If doing so does not result in a decrease of the behavior, then one might assume that he is engaging in the behavior to increase the sensory input to his system. If that's the case, then placing a Velcro strip underneath the student's desk and urging him to run his fingers over it may give him the input he craves. Adding a piece of therapy putty or a Koosh ball to his sensory diet may also replace the behavior.

Previously, self-abusive behaviors were addressed in various ways that included the use of aversive techniques, drugs, diets, and psychotherapy. Some researchers addressed self-abusive behavior by delivering a shock (with a self-injurious behavior-inhibiting system, or SIBIS) whenever the individual engaged in such behavior. Aversive techniques are controversial and are considered to be an unethical way of handling self-abusive behavior in an educational setting, and, often, little effort is put into discovering the communicative intent of such behaviors. In educational settings, it is extremely important that this behavior be addressed with the use of data collection so that the team can attempt to discover the *where, when, with whom,* and thus, the *why* of the behavior. Jane Ayres believed that "given the opportunity to do so, the brain will organize itself."[23] Thus, a student that is engaging in self-abusive behavior might indeed be an individual who is attempting to organize sensory input.

We must not forget that there may be an underlying medical condition that causes some children to engage in self-abusive or self-stimulatory behaviors, especially when there may be limited communication ability. Such conditions could include toothaches, headaches, urinary-tract infections, yeast infections, acid reflux, stomachaches, or earaches. A phone call home to the parents would be the first place to start to rule these out as possible causes for this type of behavior.

If data collection shows that times of transition or unexpected changes to routine can result in self-abusive behaviors, then visual schedules can serve as transition devices to prepare a student for changes of routine during his school day. They also serve another purpose: They provide teachable moments for students who need to learn to respond to sensory input more appropriately. In the minutes leading up to a problem module at school, stress-management techniques can be introduced and reviewed with the student. We will explore stress-management techniques in the next chapter. Appropriate stress management can increase the student's ability to function in environments that he previously found necessary to avoid. This, in turn, will help him to become more flexible and gain additional skills that lead to greater independence.

Learning about Private and Public Behavior

School is a public place. The word "public" means that there are usually people around me.

I can see other students or teachers in my class, in the restroom, in the halls, in the cafeteria, and wherever I may be in the school building. School is a public place.

My bedroom at home is a private place. The word "private" means that other people are not around me.

Often, I can be alone in my bedroom, or in my bathroom at home.

Using private behavior in pubic places is not acceptable. This includes touching my genitals. When I touch my genitals in public places, it makes people feel uncomfortable. When I am older, touching my genitals in public places may be against the law.

It may feel nice to touch my genitals, but it is not acceptable to do so at school. If other people see me doing this, it may make them laugh, become embarrassed, or even upset them.

I will try not to touch my genitals in school. Instead, I can use my fidget toys or my Koosh ball, or run my hands along the Velcro strip under my desk.

In this way, I can keep private behavior private and public behavior public.

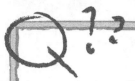

Reader Questions

1. **I have heard that there is medication that is used to stop self-abusive behavior. Is that true?** *Yes. Naltrexone is a drug used frequently to help with self-injurious behavior. It is an opiate-receptor antagonist. That means that it blocks the effects of drugs, such as codeine, heroin, and morphine. It is also used to treat alcohol addiction. Some doctors are finding that naltrexone reduces self-abusive behavior by eliminating the endorphins (or pleasure chemicals) that may result when one engages in this type of behavior. This eliminates the "rush" that the patient receives from engaging in self-injurious behavior. Thus, naltrexone also acts as an endorphin antagonist.*

2. **I have a student who recites videos to himself while working. It's rather eerie, as he can often recite the entire script, using the intonations of all the characters from the movie accurately. Could this scripting be his way of keeping himself at optimal alertness?** *Good thinking! This student may be using his echolalia (the scripting of language) to keep himself attentive. With other children, it may be a calming*

device. Some children hum or sing to themselves; others will engage in making mouth noises. For these children, it may be helpful to provide gustatory input (chewing gum, mints, candy, or water). This type of self-stimulatory behavior can certainly be distracting to peers! If the gustatory input does not help to relieve the scripting, you might consider that the student is attempting to relieve stress. It would be useful to see, with the use of data collection, if the echolalia is occurring more often in certain subjects or at certain periods of the day, and address it accordingly.

3. **My child's teachers prefer to ignore his self-stimulatory behavior. I want them to stop it, as it looks weird. What do you think?** Even behavior that "looks weird" is serving a purpose for the child. I would be hesitant to stop his behavior without a period of data collection to try to determine its communicative intent. You may instigate a behavior that is even worse than the first. It is always best to attempt to find out why the student is engaging in the behavior in the first place, and/or teach a replacement behavior that is more socially acceptable.

4. **My daughter has a great deal of difficulty**

sitting still for extended periods of time. She is always trying to find something to do with her hands. Her latest habit is to roll a piece of cellophane tape up so that it is sticky on both sides. She then affixes one side to the tip of her finger and rubs it back and forth against the tip of her finger on the opposite hand. What's going on here? *Your daughter might be trying to give herself some tactile input. Try providing her with a stress-reduction toy or a piece of Velcro under her desk so that she can rub her hands along it. You may also need to reduce the amount of time that she is required to sit.*

5. **Should children with self-injurious behavior be punished when they engage in this type of behavior?** *There's no doubt that punishers are important in the field of ABA, because for some behaviors, they can be very effective. Personally, I feel that it is important to try to discover what the behavior is communicating and possibly address it through that avenue before attempting punishment.*

Chapter 8

Teaching Stress Management and Self-Advocacy through Cognitive Behavioral Therapy

L et's face it. If we really want kids with sensory-integration problems to be able to cope in life, we simply can't devote all our planning time to finding ways to help them escape these experiences. There are always going to be moments of sensory overload that we cannot prepare for. Sometimes, the best way to teach a new skill *is to plan for what to do in these moments*. When we teach a child how to manage his stress, we are teaching a lifelong skill that he will be able to use over and over again, and not just for sensory catastrophes.

The science of ABA provides for us an important educational mandate: *Any behavior that is reinforced is likely to continue*. So, when a child receives reinforcement (reward) for problematic behavior, that behavior will most likely continue or even increase in frequency. When he receives reinforcement (reward) for preferred behavior, we can expect that behavior to continue, as well. Consider the following:

> *Jane was a fifth grader and a proficient flute player. All who heard her play felt that she had a gift. However, Jane had an overactive sensory system. When she attempted to play with her fellow band members, the noise of the other instruments was too much for her. She could*

Note: Because we are all individuals, it is helpful to consider that for some children, the process of weaning into a challenging sensory situation may be more difficult than for others. Often, there have been years of avoidance and reinforcement of escape behaviors that have to be chipped away. Some students may make slow progress. On days when the child is tired or sick or has other stressors, there may be periods of regression.

not remain seated for more than 10 minutes and frequently had to leave the room for the rest of rehearsal. Her parents were frustrated. They had paid for years of lessons, and now it appeared that Jane was going to have to quit the band. A behavioral specialist was consulted to see if there was anything that could be done to help Jane learn to tolerate the sound of the other instruments. The behavioral specialist felt that although it was a compassionate move, allowing Jane to leave the band room had inadvertently reinforced escape. Because of Jane's love for music and the social opportunities it provided, the school's occupational therapist and the behavioral specialist developed a behavior plan to wean Jane back into band. First, Jane was taught some basic stress-management techniques. These included chanting a mantra and deep breathing. Then, she was exposed to particular sounds of instruments in isolation, first through recordings, and then by actual players. She was also encouraged to try to play each instrument herself. This was a gentle form of exposure, introduced in a quiet room, under her own control, to confront the sounds she detested.

Next, Jane was exposed to a tape-recording of the entire band. For every 5 minutes that she was able to listen to it, she earned a paper "dollar." With paper "dollars," she could purchase items from the student store. Finally, Jane was weaned back into the actual band period itself for 5, 10, and 15 minutes, and then for increasing increments of time, always with reinforcement (paper "dollars") and with a review and practice session of her stress-management techniques. Eventually, the paper "dollars" were weaned away, and Jane became a full participant in band.

ABA also provides for us another instructional strategy that is useful when dealing with anxiety. This strategy is referred to as *errorless teaching*. With errorless teaching, we want the learning experience to be successful so that we can reinforce it, because *any behavior that is reinforced is likely to continue*. With academic tasks, that often means hand-over-hand support so that the student does not make a mistake and can earn the reinforcer. In Jane's case, we want all her attempts at remaining in band to be successful. Therefore, as soon as Jane enters the room, errorless teaching should begin. For Jane, that would mean she may only stay in band 5 minutes so that we can reinforce her success. Her staff members, for that brief 5 minutes, need to be her cheerleaders—encouraging her attempts, modeling stress-management techniques, and congratulating her with reinforcers frequently.

Jane's staff members rehearsed and modeled her stress strategies even before she entered the room. She was provided with a paper "dollar" as she entered the room and another as she took her seat. If the selected reinforcers are powerful enough for Jane, she will remain in band, because it is more reinforcing for her to be there than to leave. An important part of this plan was to make sure that the paper "dollars" would be reinforcing to Jane. The paper "dollars" served as *intermittent reinforcers.* Intermittent reinforcers are given to children when it is not feasible to give the primary reinforcer. Often, intermittent reinforcers can "tide" a child over until the actual reinforcer can be delivered. Since the actual reinforcer was something she could purchase from the student store, it was important that Jane first identified something from the store that she was working toward earning. If there was nothing in the store that interested her, then the intermittent reinforcers would be useless. Many educators make the mistake of choosing a reinforcer that *they* feel is appropriate for the child to earn. If the student is not interested in that reinforcer, it is doubtful that the corresponding behavioral plan will work.

Jane's staff members started with 5 minutes as the length of exposure in band. They were comfortable with choosing 5 minutes because of the success they had achieved previously with having her listen to a tape-recording of the band for much longer periods of time. As an additional accommodation, Jane was provided with earplugs that she could insert if she needed to muffle the sound somewhat. Because Jane was such a talented musician, even wearing earplugs did not interfere with her playing. If she could hear some of the music, she knew where her cues were to begin playing. She often only wore the earplugs when the selections were too loud.

One thing that we have not discussed at this point is self-esteem. When a child is able to tackle the things that disturb him and utilize a set of learned strategies to cope, he begins to build a sense of self-confidence. We know that kids who have healthy self-esteem also have self-confidence. The bricks that a child lays when he conquers his fears are the foundation for future successes. For some children who are moving into middle-school and high-school years, sensory-processing problems have often caused them to withdraw from activities that would be great social outlets for them. Thus, they retreat to their homes, away from the things that cause them stress, and they gain no replacement skills that would help them deal with future confrontations of sensory challenges. Escaping sensory overload becomes the primary way of dealing with it. Many adults with sensory dysfunction report that they handle the challenges associated with this disorder better now that they are older, compared with the way they handled them as youngsters. It is doubtful that they grew out of their problem. What most likely happened instead was that they learned to *tolerate their disorder* by using whatever behavioral or emotional strategies they acquired along the way.

> *William was a 4-year-old boy who hated denim, corduroy, and twill pants. He would have a tantrum if he was required to wear anything other than sweatpants. His wardrobe was becoming a problem for occasions such as weddings, funerals, and church services. The behaviors he exhibited went far beyond a preference for the sweatpants. He would scream, cry, and sometimes become violent if asked to wear any other types of clothing. A behavioral specialist was consulted about the problem. She encouraged the family to provide exposure to William by having him earn computer time for every minute he was able to wear the pants around his ankles, calves, knees, and finally his hips. Computer time was highly reinforcing for him. Today, as an adult, William will tell you that he still dislikes denim. He is now able to attend his college classes while wearing jeans, just as the other students do. When class is over, he returns to his dorm and changes into the clothes he prefers. William has been provided*

with cognitive behavioral therapy—therapy that has enabled him, through exposure in small doses, to master his anxiety disorder.

Besides behavioral management, there are also strategies that are useful for teaching stress management to children with sensory disturbances.

First and foremost, it is important that a student be made aware of upcoming sensory challenges while he learns stress-management techniques. For this reason, visual schedules are extremely important. Occasionally, parents will remark, "My child is so stressed in school! He is completely wiped out when he comes home and often unleashes his frustration on us." Kids who are bombarded with offensive sensory moments will indeed have increased frustration levels. Sometimes they will be able to cope with them, and sometimes they will not. Their home is often their "safe place" to vent and to unwind. School personnel may not recognize the degree of their frustration, as some children hide internal stress well. For this reason, visual schedules often "get the child ready" for whatever it is that is coming, and reviewing the schedule presents a teachable moment to review and prepare a strategy for the upcoming assault to their senses.

Kids need to learn how to take care of their own wants and needs. Staff members should model strategies to stay calm before the event occurs. Modeling the same strategies "in the moment" is even better. Therefore, this will require a collaborative effort among staff members and parents for consistency. Rewarding appropriate behavior as the student demonstrates it "in the moment" will help to reinforce new skills. We can't teach stress-management techniques at the same time the child is experiencing sensory overload, as he will most likely be too challenged by the stimuli to be able to assimilate any new ways of dealing with it. Therefore, proactive teaching is important.

Deep-breathing techniques are often core components of

many methods of relaxation. Children who are stressed often hyperventilate. Their breathing is shallow, and although they can feel the air going into their noses, their lungs barely expand. Teaching the child to close his eyes and take 15 to 20 slow breaths in a quiet area will help him feel more grounded.

It is helpful to use some sort of visual to encourage deep breathing when a child is out of sorts. One recommended visual is a glitter bottle. Instructions for making these bottles will be provided at the end of this chapter. Glitter bottles contain Karo syrup, glitter, sequins, and beads. As the child is learning to inhale and exhale properly, the bottle can be tilted to allow a slow flow of Karo syrup to the other side. As he tilts the bottle, he should inhale slowly, breathing in deeply. Once the Karo has left the one side of the bottle and gathered at the other end, the child can tilt the bottle in the opposite direction and begin to exhale slowly as the Karo moves to the opposite end. The process can be repeated as needed until the child can keep his breathing slow and purposeful.

During times of stress, the glitter bottle can be presented to the child. As he watches the Karo glitter solution flow to the opposite end of the tilted bottle, he can be prompted to concentrate on the movement and slow his breathing down to match.

Another useful technique is to teach the child *a mantra*. Mantras are simple affirmations, but when chanted over and over, often become thought-changing tools! Most of us can remember the story of *The Little Engine That Could*.[24] Providing a student with a similar calming phrase ("I think I can! I think I can!") that he can recite to himself repetitiously before a sensory-challenging event is about to occur can indeed make a huge difference in the way he perceives these moments.

One young boy detested physical-education classes. His coordination was lacking, his eyes did not team well with his limbs, and he suffered from auditory sensitivity. Thus, P.E. was frequently a class that would send him into sensory overload. His parents taught him some stress-management techniques, and one of the things they found most useful was teaching him to recite a mantra to himself. The mantra was, "I can handle it because I'm flexible!" The boy's parents shared the mantra with their son's teachers. The teachers began to review the mantra and some deep-breathing techniques with the student prior to each P.E. class. They also developed a behavioral plan that incorporated a reward system for appropriate behavior and alternative activities for the boy to do in P.E. with some peers if the activity was too hard for him. When it appeared that the boy was coping, the P.E. teacher reinforced his appropriate behavior with wooden nickels—an intermittent reinforcer that earned him time with Legos. It wasn't too long before the boy was not only participating in P.E., but doing so without incident. What is important to remember is that the student's P.E. teacher realized that he did not have the athletic ability to do some of the activities in P.E. Thus, the modifications he made to the activities also significantly reduced the boy's stress level.

So many times, teachers forget that sensory disturbances sometimes require classroom modifications, as well. The example above is a case in point. If you can't coordinate your body to serve a volleyball, you will continually be a liability to your teammates. Often this will result in social problems for the student, as well. Therefore, having the student serve as the scorekeeper or the referee instead of directly participating in such activities would certainly reduce his stress level, without reinforcing escape from those activities. Oftentimes, including the student in the planning of the activity is useful. When a student can learn to self-advocate for needed supports, this, too, will help build self-esteem and confidence. Teaching the child to self-advocate is important so that he doesn't become dependent on adults and unable to solve his own problems.

Figure 15. Biodots can be placed on the fingertips to help a child recognize when he is starting to experience stress. Once he sees the color change, he can self-advocate and seek the support he needs.

Another technique that might be useful to teach with regard to stress management is *guided imagery*. Frequently, when a child needs to decompress, he might be encouraged to listen to soft music or to engage in something that is less stimulating. *Guided imagery* is a form of self-meditation, where the student literally pictures himself, through his imagination, in a place or time that is pleasurable to him. Showing the child a photo or picture of a lush, tropical beach or a restful forest scene and having him concentrate on actually being in that scene is sometimes very helpful. Some educators pair restful pictures with sounds—for instance, a tabletop fountain paired with a picture of a small brook gently flowing through a forest. Once the student has mastered the skill in a one-on-one setting, his staff members may be able to expose him to brief occasions of sensory-overload situations because he has mastered the concept of guided imagery.

As was mentioned previously, aerobic exercise appears to be of benefit for some children prior to occasions where sensory overload is expected. When your heart is pumping, endorphins are flowing! Those endorphins are what our bodies need to fight stress. Many fitness experts cite the benefits of exercise to reduce stress, and there is much research to support this concept.

There is a new product on the market today to help children

recognize their stress levels. Biodots are small, heat-sensitive dots that can be stuck to a fingertip (**Figure 15**). When an individual is tense, the temperature of his fingertips may drop. Often this small change in temperature is not even detected by the individual. The dots, however, can detect the change. They change color and let the wearer know that she is experiencing stress.

Biodots help to teach children to recognize when the "fight-or-flight" response is eminent so that they are able to seek out needed support before their stress reaches disproportionate levels. The fight-or-flight response is a primitive reaction to our body's awareness that we are in danger. When we experience extreme stress, blood rushes away from areas where it is not needed to areas where it is needed more, such as our limbs and muscles. Our pupils begin to dilate. Through the lens of fear, we see everyone and everything as a possible threat to our existence. It is not possible for us to reason under such anxiety, and often, our thoughts become distorted or irrational. So it is with children who experience sensory overload. Oftentimes, children cannot communicate what they need before they become too bombarded to realize they are experiencing overload. When the Biodots change color, the student will be able to "see" her stress, as will the adults working with her. Biodots are available at *www.cliving.org*.

Another strategy for helping children learn to self-advocate is provided by the How Does Your Engine Run program (frequently referred to as the Alert Program). The Alert Program teaches a child to recognize where his engine (ie, attention level) is at in terms of engine speed. "Engines" that are running too high need calming sensory activities. "Engines" that are running too slow need revving-up activities. Having a child identify where

1	2	3
Too slow!	Just right!	Too fast!
Stretch	Proceed	Take a deep breath
Eat a mint		Squeeze my stress-reduction toy
Get a drink		Visit the tent

his engine is running on a continuum during different times of the day may be helpful. A visual display of the continuum is also helpful for youngsters, with corresponding strategies to try:

The author has also written a book *(Addressing the Challenging Behaviors of Students with High-Functioning Autism/Asperger's Syndrome in the Classroom)* that describes the use of another visual to gauge stress levels. A barometer is marked off at different "degrees," with strategies to use as the student's stress level elevates. During different prearranged times of the day, the student is asked to identify the reading of his barometer gauge, and then he is reminded to implement the appropriate strategies for the level identified.[25]

Teachers who are proactive about allowing children to advocate for sensory-diet items and permit them to engage with these in the classroom to regulate their attention levels will in turn have kids that can achieve optimal on-task behavior. They will also have at their disposal a powerful way to help children with sensory challenges learn to deal with their deficits without exhibiting meltdown behaviors.

Making A Glitter Bottle

What you will need:

Clear Karo syrup

Sequins

Small, brightly colored beads

Glitter (any color)

Empty water bottle

Super glue

Directions:

Pour the Karo syrup into an empty water bottle until it's about ¼ full. Drop some beads and sequins into the bottle. Add some glitter. Super-glue the lid onto the bottle, as the contents are very sticky and you do not want them to spill!

Tilt or shake the bottle to mix the contents. (**Figure 16**).

Figure 16. A glitter bottle is easy to make and provides a good visual to encourage deep breathing when a child is out of sorts. Tilt the bottle and have the child inhale slowly. Once the Karo has gathered at one end of the bottle, tilt the bottle in the opposite direction, and have the child exhale slowly as the Karo moves to the opposite end. This process can be repeated as needed until the child can keep his breathing slow and purposeful.

Reader Questions

1. One of our students has auditory sensitivity. We have been so careful to avoid having him participate in loud assemblies. We remove him from the building prior to fire drills. When we see him cover his ears, we rush to his aid. I am worried about how he is going to cope in middle school. He is in the fourth grade and will be transitioning to middle school in sixth grade. How will he cope with class changes when the bell rings two times in between each class? I don't mean to sound cruel, but shouldn't we be "toughening him up?"

   Well, it depends on what you mean by "toughening him up." You raise a valid concern about how he is going to cope in the future if he is allowed to escape these sensory disturbances. However, what your school team should consider is providing him with accommodations (headphones or hats) to muffle the sound, and stress-management techniques to utilize when he is experiencing sensory overload. If we want him to be able to survive in middle school, we are going to have to teach him coping mechanisms. What you don't want to do is yank the supports you have put in place while this is happening.

2. I have heard that cognitive behavioral

therapy is useful in addressing anxiety issues. It seems to me that SPD may also be related to anxiety, and thus this type of "talking therapy" may be helpful for some kids. Do you think this is true? *Absolutely! Although basic "talking therapy" is helpful for some people, cognitive behavioral therapy takes the extra step: It teaches patients what to do to help themselves. Cognitive behavioral therapy would certainly blend nicely with any kind of sensory-integration techniques you use. It works even better when an occupational therapist and a mental-health therapist work together to overcome sensory-related anxiety.*

Chapter 9
IEP and 504 Language for SPD

As stated earlier in this book, a child could qualify for an IEP, provided his team agrees that he has a disability and that the disability requires special-education services. The IEP could then afford the child sensory-integration accommodations.

Many times, goals for SPD are not included in the IEP. However, if the team attempts to eliminate behavioral problems that they feel are related to sensory-processing difficulties, these goals can be written in measurable wording so that data can be collected to determine progress. The following are examples:

> *Using a sensory diet, Matthew will decrease the number of outbursts related to sensory disturbances from an average of six per week to fewer than three per week.*

Or:

> *Matthew will demonstrate the ability to put stress-management strategies into practice and diffuse meltdowns during difficult sensory moments (P.E., music, and recess) in eight out of 10 observable occasions.*

If accommodations and adaptations are helping the child to be successful, then clearly, the data collection associated with these goals would reflect an improvement in the child's behavior.

Different states have different section titles within their IEP pages, but all states should have a page that lists the specially designed instruction items or accommodations that would need to be provided in the classroom for a child with SPD. They could include any of the following:

A. Preferential seating. (The team should determine the best place for him to sit in the classroom, on the basis of his particular needs, to allow for optimal attention. Questions to be asked may include: Which peers should not be seated with this student? Where does he need to be in relationship to the teacher? What areas in the classroom are going to be problematic for him? What is the arrangement of the desks—single or table style? Would being seated in high-traffic areas near the garbage can or pencil sharpener, for instance, be a problem for him?)

B. Sensory diet. (The team should specify what items are going to be acceptable in the diet and at what times the student should be provided with such items. For instance, let's say the child will be provided with Thera-Bands on his chair rungs. This should be listed on the IEP. If he moves to other rooms during the day, then the team needs to write the locations where this intervention will be incorporated. If the team agrees to allow stress-reduction toys, be sure to state when and where they will be included, as well. Sensory-diet items may include seat cushions, weighted vests, weighted lap pads, stress-reduction toys, water bottles, chewing gum, mints, sunglasses, hoodies, drinking straws, lotions, lip balm, etc.)

C. Advance warning of fire alarms. (For some children with extreme auditory sensitivity, this is critical.)

D. De-stress time in the sensory room. (Writing in the IEP that she will be given an opportunity to visit the sensory room before certain subject areas or after times that are challenging for her and specifically naming those times is important!)

E. Opportunity for movement. (Writing in the IEP that the child should be provided with aerobic exercise for 15 minutes during a specific time of the day would give fidgety children a way to get rid of excess energy so that they can concentrate on their schoolwork. Another accommodation would be to write that sitting time will be limited to 15-minute segments. In addition, perhaps the student could be provided with movement activities of daily errands to the office twice each day.)

F. Physical-education accommodations. (Writing that the child will serve as the referee, scorekeeper, or supply coordinator instead of engaging in competitive sports, or noting that teams will be selected in an A-B-A-B fashion rather than by peer selection, can help to eliminate embarrassment. It might also be useful to note that some activities in P.E. should be modified if they require eye/hand coordination.)

G. Use of earplugs. (For example, a student will be allowed to use them at lunch or recess or during music periods if he feels he needs them.)

Note: The environment of a bus is frequently a nightmare situation for kids with SPD. School districts sometimes have difficulty seeing that handling bus problems falls within their jurisdiction. Often, transportation is subcontracted to local businesses. However, the school district still retains control over what happens on the bus. Legally, they are responsible for their students' safety and well-being. Children with disabilities are afforded transportation. As such, accommodations required as part of that transportation are part of IDEA Related Services. Kids with SPD may have several types of accommodations. Some of these might include assigned seating, being allowed to use an ipod or video game to help distract them from overwhelming stimuli, taxi services, smaller buses, shorter bus rides, bus rides with or without disabled students, and alternative seating arrangements (one child per seat, instead of two or three).

H. Assigned seating on the bus. (Certain environments are especially challenging for some children. Assigning a seat on the bus or in the cafeteria can provide a sense of calm for some students.)

I. Use of latex-free gloves for completing messy projects. (These can be useful in some classes, such as art or science.)

J. A visual schedule of the student's day. (It's critical that this be reviewed with the student at the start of the day and referred to frequently, especially when there is going to be a change.)

K. Instruction and rehearsal of stress-management strategies. (Again, it helps to be as specific as possible about the types of stress-management techniques that are going to be utilized. Examples might be the use of mantras, Biodots, deep breathing, or a stress-level chart to help the student identify his stress level, etc.)

L. Establishment of a de-stress area in the classroom.

M. Establishment of a de-stress area in the school.

N. Use of a cool-down pass. (When a student needs to leave the room, he can present this pass, and he will not be questioned.)

O. An alternative area for eating lunch. (If the team decides the child is not ready to handle the sensory demands of the cafeteria, then deciding how he is going to eat and where will be necessary.)

P. Weaning into sensory stressful times and/or areas with reinforcement.

Q. Use of a communication book that is shared with parents, detailing problematic behaviors. (Where, when, what, and with whom.)

R. Data collection of problem behaviors, using a line graph with the frequency and a description of the subject or task being completed at the time.

The Related Services section of the IEP is useful for students with SPD. Related Services are services that are provided to the student. These services could include:

A. Occupational therapy. (Occupational therapy can be consultative or direct. Consultative therapy is when the occupational therapist makes recommendations for sensory-integration techniques to be utilized in the classroom. In other words, the therapist spends more time as a consultant, rather than as someone who devotes hands-on time to the student. Direct therapy is one-on-one therapy with the student. Both types, consultative and direct, need to include detailed descriptions of how often they are going to occur and for what lengths of time.)

B. A classroom aide to help implement those techniques. (It will be important, again, to indicate whether this is an aide assigned to the student, a shared aide, or a classroom aide.)

C. Behavioral support specialist. (The role of this individual would be to track and analyze data about sensory-related behaviors, as well as to create classroom accommodations and modifications and incorporate those into a positive behavioral support plan. The frequency with which this individual should be consulted should be noted in the IEP.)

Note: In most states, Specially Designed Instruction (Accommodations) and Related Services require specific language and avoidance of the use of words such as "as needed" or "at teacher discretion" or "when necessary." Such wording is not helpful in determining, specifically, when these services should be implemented. Often, if they are not written in a time-sensitive manner, they may not be used at all or very sparingly. This can certainly reduce their effectiveness in the classroom.

D. Guidance counselor or "safe person." (This is a great person to serve as the instructor of stress-management techniques, as well as someone the student can seek out when things are getting rough. The safe person can serve as a facilitator between the parents and the classroom teachers. The frequency with which the child will meet with the safe person and that person's name should be listed in the IEP.)

Another section of the IEP that is useful for including sensory-integration support is the section titled, "Supports for Personnel." This section is meant to list all supports that will be provided for the teacher or those who work with the student. Some examples for this section may include:

A. The first week of school, a parent will meet with the staff for ½ hour to brief them about the student's sensory difficulties.

B. An occupational therapist will consult with classroom teachers one time per week.

C. A behavioral support specialist will consult with classroom teachers one time per week.

D. The teacher will be provided with a minimum of 3 hours of in-service training on sensory integration during the first 9 weeks of school. (Parents: If you have found a great DVD or video depicting sensory-integration techniques, you could purchase it for the district and request that the teachers view it as a requirement for their training.)

E. A teacher's aide will be provided with 3 hours of in-service training on sensory integration during the first 9 weeks of school.

The Americans with Disabilities Act allows children with disabilities who do not meet the criteria for special-education services to receive accommodations that they need to be successful in their school settings. The document that is developed as a result of this law is commonly referred to as a 504 document. Accommodations that could be written into such a document include any of the examples the author has provided here, as well as any of the Related Service or Supports for Personnel suggestions. 504 plans do not contain student goals or objectives. Thus, they are not designed to measure progress. A 504 document's purpose is to "level the playing field" for a child who has a disability that is recognized by the district, when the district agrees that this disability substantially affects one or more of his major life functions. When a district recognizes a child's disability but does not agree that he requires special-education services, a 504 is often provided in lieu of an IEP.

Occasionally, school personnel believe that a 504 document is not as enforceable as an IEP document. IEPs are enforceable under special-education law (IDEA), and 504s are enforceable under the Americans with Disabilities Act. Failure to provide specially designed instruction, supports, and services in accordance with an IEP is failure to provide a free and appropriate education. Failure to provide accommodations under a 504 is viewed as discrimination toward a handicapped person.

IEP documents and 504 plans are meant to provide specific instructions in the way a student with a disability should be educated. They are developed as a team effort, with parents, administrators, and teachers brainstorming the ways in which a child can be successful in his classroom environment. With careful thought and attention, they are wonderful roadmaps that will enable a child to progress to his maximum potential alongside his peers.

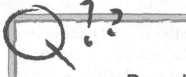

Reader Questions

1. **I just can't get my school's IEP team to buy into the idea that sensory-integration techniques can be useful. Any ideas on what I can do?** *If your child is exhibiting any sort of behavior that is impeding his learning or the learning of others, write a letter to your school's special-education director, requesting a functional behavioral assessment. The reason why you must write the letter is because the letter drives certain procedures: They will send you a permission notice to conduct evaluation, as well as parent-input forms. When you return those forms, the district must complete this evaluation within a certain number of days. Oral requests may not be honored. On your parent-input forms, it will be necessary to document that you believe your child suffers from SPD, and explain why. The district should make every attempt to consider your input and evaluate your child's problem, even if that means bringing in an expert in sensory integration.*

2. **My child doesn't qualify for occupational**

therapy. **Is this the only way I can get sensory-integration techniques in my child's classroom?** *No! Any accommodations that a team feels are necessary can be included and written into the IEP.*

3. **My child is moving on to seventh grade next year. The team wants to remove his sensory-room privileges and fidget toys, as they say he needs to become more independent. What do you think?** *For some children, taking away these supports may be the equivalent of not allowing you to wear your glasses or contact lenses. Just because a child reaches a certain age does not mean that these supports are not needed. Only after a period of data collection proves they are no longer necessary should you agree to do this.*

Chapter 10

A Behavioral Support Plan for Children with SPD

The following behavioral support plan was written for a student with SPD.

Demographics
Name of student: *Michael Daily*
Grade: *10th Grade*
Parents: *Michelle and Robert Daily*
Phone: *262-528-2006*

Date: *March 4, 2010*
Implementation Date: *March 5, 2010*

Description of the Student's Behavior *Michael is a friendly 10th-grade boy with a specific learning disability in math. He enjoys computers and video games. During various times of the school day, he slaps his head, his thighs, and his face. Sometimes the slaps will be light; at other times, the slaps will be loud and leave a red mark. Michael also suffers from headaches, which his parents believe are* *attributed to stress. The behavior of concern began at the beginning of the school year, with a frequency of two or three times per week. However, as of the second marking period, it has increased to an average of four or five times daily.*

Antecedents *A functional behavioral assessment was conducted, and the resulting data helped the team to determine that the following types of triggers exist:*

- *Math worksheets – Michael is a 10th grader, but functions on a 2nd-grade level in this subject area. The math module had the highest number or slaps.*

- *Unexpected changes to routines*

- *Loud, noisy environments*

- *Illness or days when Michael is not feeling well*

Replacement Behavior *Michael needs to learn self-advocacy tools to ask for what he needs: help in math, use of headphones when it is too noisy, visiting the nurse when he is sick, or requesting a break when needed.*

Antecedent Strategies

1. *Michael's math teacher will make sure that all math worksheets and tests are given in accordance with his ability level. Michael will be provided with manipulatives at his desk, as well as a*

calculator. Michael will not participate in timed math activities and will take his tests in a quiet area of the room.

2. Michael will be provided with a visual schedule of his day. His homeroom teacher will review the schedule with Michael each morning prior to the start of classes. His individual classroom teachers will remind him throughout the day if a change to his schedule is coming up.

3. The guidance counselor will work with Michael one time per week during his study-hall period to teach Michael self-advocacy skills and stress-management techniques. He will detail what he is doing after each session in an e-mail to all of his teachers, as well as to Michael's parents. In this way, his teachers and parents can review and practice the same strategies with Michael when he appears to be getting stressed "in the moment."

4. Michael will be provided with a set of earplugs that he can place discreetly in his ears when his environment is getting too noisy. Each classroom teacher will also be provided with an extra set of these earplugs, in case Michael does not have them with him when he needs them.

5. Because Michael suffers from tension headaches, he will be provided with a nurse's pass that he can use as needed.

6. *A sensory-deprivation time will be provided on Michael's schedule, to occur immediately after lunch (a sensory-overload time for him). After Michael eats his lunch, he will report to the sensory room for the last 10 minutes of the lunch period prior to his math class. The sensory-deprivation area will consist of a large beanbag chair, a CD player with a disk of nature sounds or classical music, and a pair of headphones for listening privately.*

Consequences When the Student Engages in an Inappropriate Behavior *Michael will be redirected to use a stress-reduction toy or Theraputty when he begins to hit himself. He will be reminded by staff members to engage in his stress-management practices and/or to self-advocate for what he needs.*

Consequences When the Student Engages in an Appropriate Behavior *For every class in which Michael does not hit himself, he will earn a check mark on his daily behavior card. Each check mark represents 1 minute of computer time. Michael will receive his computer time in his study-hall period at the end of the day.*

Measurement of Progress *Michael's team will record data by using a frequency count, along with a summary of what is going on in the classroom when the behavior occurs. Data collection will continue for a 3-week period* *following the implementation of the plan. The team will reconvene after the 3rd week if a reduction in the behaviors has not occurred.*

References

1. Willey L. *Pretending to be Normal.* London, England: Jessica Kingsley Publishers; 1999.

2. Ayres AJ. *Sensory Integration and Learning Disorders.* Los Angeles, CA: Western Psychological Services; 1972.

3. Ayres AJ. *Sensory Integration and the Child.* Los Angeles, CA: Western Psychological Services; 2005 (reprint).

4. Ayres AJ. Sensory Integration Praxis Test. Los Angeles, CA: Western Psychological Services; 1988.

5. Knickerbocker BM. *A Holistic Approach to the Treatment of Learning Disabilities.* Thorofare, NJ: C. B. Slack; 1980.

6. Grandin T. *Emergence: Labeled Autistic.* New York, NY: Warner Books; 1996.

7. Grandin T. *Thinking in Pictures and Other Reports from my Life with Autism.* New York, NY: Doubleday Publishers; 1995.

8. Barron S, Barron J. *There's a Boy in Here.* Arlington, TX: Future Horizons; 1992.

9. SPD Foundation. Understanding sensory processing disorder and recent research in ASD. Presented at: 10th Annual National Autism Conference; July 30–August 3, 2007; State College, PA. http://www.google.com/search?hl=en&ie=ISO-8859-1&q=Prevelance+of+gifted+and+talented+with+significant+SPD&btnG=Google+Search. Accessed January 14, 2008.

10. Moonlial J. *Information Processing, Psychosocial Adjustment, and Sensory Processing in Gifted Youth* [dissertation]. Azusa, CA: Azusa Pacific University; 2007.

11. Greenspan S, Weider S. *The Child with Special Needs.* Cambridge, MA: Da Capo Press; 1998.

12. Individuals with Disabilities Education Act and Individuals with Disabilities Education Improvement Act, 1997, Public Law 105–17.

13. David S. A case study of sensory affective disorder in adult psychiatry. *Am Occup Ther Assoc Sensory Integration Special Interest Newsletter.* 1990;13(4): 1–4.

14. Ayres AJ, Tickle LS. Hyper-responsivity to touch and vestibular stimuli as a predictor of positive response to sensory integration procedures. *Am J Occup Ther.* 1980;34:375–381.

15. Edelson SM, Edelson MG, Kerr DC, Grandin T. Behavioral and physiological effects of deep pressure on children with autism: a pilot study evaluating the efficacy of Grandin's Hug Machine. *Am J Occup Ther.* 1999;53(2):145–152.

16. Stagnitti K, Raison P, Ryan P. Sensory defensiveness syndrome: a paediatric perspective and case study. *Aust Occup Ther J.* 1999;46:157–187.

17. Case-Smith J, Bryan T. The effects of occupational therapy with sensory integration emphasis on preschool-age children with autism. *Am J Occup Ther.* 1999;53(5):489–497.

18. Kranowitz C. *The Out of Sync Child: Recognizing and Coping with Sensory Integration Dysfunction.* New York, NY: Penguin Group; 2005:45.

19. Dunn W, Daniels D. The Sensory Profile. San Antonio, TX: Therapy Skill Builders; 1999.

20. Yack E, Sutton S, Aquilla P. *Building Bridges through Sensory Integration.* Arlington, TX: Future Horizons; 1998:18.

21. Shellenberger S, Williams M. *How Does Your Engine Run: The Alert Program for Self-Regulation.* Albuquerque, NM: Therapy Works; 1994.

22. Moyes R. *Incorporating Social Goals in the Classroom—A Guide for Teachers and Parents of Students with High-Functioning Autism and Asperger's Syndrome.* London, England: Jessica Kingley Publishers; 2001.

23. Ayres AJ. *Sensory Integration and the Child.* Los Angeles, CA: Western Psychological Services; 1979.

24. Piper W. *The Little Engine That Could.* New York, NY: Penguin Books; 2005.

25. Moyes R. *Addressing the Challenging Behavior of Children with High-Functioning Autism/Asperger's Syndrome in the Classroom.* London, England: Jessica Kingsley Publishers; 2002.

About the Author

R ebecca is a former education teacher in public and private schools for nine years and is the author of six books for educators who teach students with special needs. She has a master's in teaching and curriculum with an emphasis on special-needs children. She also holds an autism certificate in PA and advanced training in applied behavior analysis. She has trained educators and parents in 43 states and in Canada. Becky served on the Autism Task Force in Pennsylvania under Governor Ridge. She has also worked as a behavior consultant and trainer for several districts in Pennsylvania, as well as in Tennessee, Illinois, Maine, and Kansas.

Becky currently is the founder and director of Grade Point Resources, a Pittsburgh area corporation that focuses on providing resources, training, and services for special needs students to school districts and private schools. Rebecca has created a life skills classroom model that is currently being implemented in three school districts, as well as two private schools.

Becky can be reached via email at bmoyes123@aol.com for consultation and/or training requests.

Resources

Sensory World is the world's largest publisher devoted exclusively to resources for those interested in sensory processing disorder. They also sponsor national conferences for parents, teachers, therapists, and others interested in supporting those with sensory processing disorder. Visit *www.sensoryworld.com* for further information.

Phone: 817.277.0727
Toll free: 800.489.0727
Fax: 817.277.2270
E-mail: info@sensoryworld.com
www.sensoryworld.com

CPSIA information can be obtained
at www.ICGtesting.com
Printed in the USA
JSHW021352110920
7736JS00004B/9